S0-CPS-838

THE
CYCLE
JUMPERS

MARSHALL SPIEGEL

SCHOLASTIC BOOK SERVICES
New York Toronto London Auckland Sydney Tokyo

For the cooperation, assistance, and encouragement which made this book possible, the author wishes to thank Miss Susan Patricia McElynn, Baldwin, New York; Mr. Robert Quay, Phoenix, Arizona; Mr. Duane Unkefer, Milwaukee, Wisconsin; Mr. and Mrs. Ralph Gary Wells, Sr., Houston, Texas; the Fanfare Corporation, Hollywood, California; and, of course, Mr. Robert Craig Knievel and Mr. Ralph Gary Wells, Jr.

PHOTOS page 6, 19, 26-27, 34-35, 53, 64-65, 73 (top), 74, 75, 76, 77, 78-79, 84-85, and 169 — courtesy of Harley-Davidson Motor company.

PHOTOS pages 92-93, 113, 115, 116, 117 (bottom), 118, 119, 129, 137, 140, 149, 150-151, 159 courtesy of Mrs. Ralph Wells, Sr.

This book is sold subject to the condition that it shall not be resold, lent, or otherwise circulated in any binding or cover other than that in which it is published — unless prior written permission has been obtained from the publisher — and without a similar condition, including this condition, being imposed on the subsequent purchaser.

Copyright © 1973 by Scholastic Magazines, Inc. All rights reserved. Published by Scholastic Book Services, a division of Scholastic Magazines, Inc.

7th printing .... January 1975
Printed in U.S.A.

Evel Knievel is exciting to watch. People pay a great deal of money to see him do his amazing stunts. But Evel Knievel is a *professional* performer. That means he does not take risks for the fun of it. It means that he plans his stunts very carefully. He has the best of equipment and the right people to help him. Even so, things sometimes go wrong and he gets hurt. He knows that what he is doing is dangerous, and he tries his highly skilled best not to get hurt.

What he does is not something to be tried by amateurs. Like a trapeze artist, he is thrilling to watch but dangerous to try and imitate. Anyone who would take such risks "for the fun of it" would be stupid.

So watch Evel Knievel, read about him, and enjoy his skill, but do not try his stunts on your bike. To get seriously hurt is no fun at all.

CONTENTS

Page

1st CHAPTER

The King
and The Kid

THE PAGES OF HISTORY are highlighted with the feats of a special breed of men — men who have dared to challenge the unknown; men who have faced extraordinary danger;

Photo by: Marshall Spiegel

men who have ascended above their fellow men
to accomplish what appears to be the impossible. This is the story of two such men of our
time: Evel Knievel, the father of long-range
motorcycle jumping and the undisputed king
of modern day daredevils; and fifteen-year-old
Gary Wells, the kid who now challenges the
king for his crown.

7

Almost seven years ago, Evel Knievel first jumped his motorcycle for an audience over a long line of trucks. Much has happened in his life since then. Almost immediately, people were fascinated by the handsome daredevil from Butte, Montana, and word of his fantastic feats spread throughout the country. Not only did he jump his motorcycle over unbelievable hurdles — long lines of cars and trucks — but he did it with a special brand of showmanship. The public was enchanted by the man with the rhyming name who sneered arrogantly at danger and truly defied death.

But it was more than just his performances that captured the nation's imagination. Evel Knievel is a born promoter with a natural flair for attracting attention. To climb upon a motorcycle and do what has never been done before is enough in itself to draw huge crowds of spectators. But to do it in gleaming white riding leathers on a specially painted cycle, with his own air of bravado and defiance, gave Knievel the image of a knight in shining armor going forth to face a frightening dragon.

And those who saw him jump loved it all. With careful timing and well chosen words, he made his pre-jump announcements to the crowds who came to watch, preparing them for his moment of truth. He skillfully built up the suspense and the excitement. Then he mounted his machine and fired it up so that its roar was all that could be heard by the hushed crowd. He revved up his speed on the approach path and aimed for the high take-off ramp and, at the last second, veered away from it only to return again and again until he was ready . . . until he felt just right . . . until the crowd was tingling with expectation. And then he sped effortlessly up the ramp at 85 miles per hour and flew unbelievably high into the air, soaring birdlike above the cars and trucks below. And then he landed, his rear wheel crashing frighteningly on the landing ramp. He teetered there for a moment, struggling to keep his balance. And, finally, he brought the front wheel down and stopped the bike safely. Each and every performance was breathtaking and, as time went on and the length of his jumps increased, the Evel Knievel legend grew.

There were those who called him crazy and were convinced that he really wanted to kill himself. Others were certain that he'd quit as soon as he crashed and got his first lumps. Many, who heard of his performances but never saw him jump, were skeptical, convinced that no one could really jump a motorcycle that high and that far. But to Evel Knievel himself back in those early days of his career, the important thing was that people were talking about him. The more people talked, the

9

more they came to see him jump. And the more people that came, the more money he got for each appearance. A hundred people who know Evel Knievel might offer a hundred different reasons why he began jumping and why he continues after what has happened to him these past seven years. But somewhere in each of these reasons will be money, for the strange and dangerous career he has chosen for himself has been his escape from poverty and from mediocrity.

Since his first public appearance almost seven years ago, Evel Knievel has known success and failure; victory and defeat; glory and pain. He has completed more than 200 public jumps, some more spectacular than others, but all great enough and dangerous enough to end his life had his luck run out. It is difficult to believe that he has survived some of the spectacular crashes that blot his record. But they were inevitable, even for Evel Knievel. A dozen times he smashed to the ground when his landings were less than perfect. But a dozen failures in more than 200 attempts is still an enviable record.

Until recently, Knievel was the only motorcycle jumper of note. Thus, he set all the records and each time he exceeded his previous effort, a new record was set. Cycle jumping was his creation. He was its designer. He was its innovator. And for a long time, he was its only performer. The world was enchanted by the fearless stuntman on the flying motorcycle. Books, songs, and stories were written about his amazing feats. A motion picture of his life added further to his fame and fortune.

Each of his public jumps was a spectacular performance. He thrilled 99,000 people at the Houston (Texas) Astrodome, where he jumped over 19 Dodge Colts lined up side by side. At Pocono (Pennsylvania) Raceway, he crashed painfully after a daring leap that ended with a bad landing. Early last year, at the "Cycle-Rama '71" in Chicago's International Amphitheater, he cleared a mere 10 cars, but thrilled the fans nonetheless for beneath the 18-foot ceiling he had only 12 inches of headroom! The list of his amazing leaps seems endless. He's done "his thing" across the nation — at Ontario (California) Motor Speedway; at the San Francisco (California) Cow Palace; at Seattle (Washington) International Raceway; and at Caesar's Palace, the famous hotel and gambling casino in Las Vegas, Nevada.

Of all his jumps to date, Evel Knievel must count the Caesar's Palace leap as his most notable. It was there that he jumped the farthest and it was there, in a spectacular crash, that he was most seriously hurt. The jump measured 144 feet six inches, longer and higher

11

than anyone had ever dreamed a man could fly a motorcycle. It was a record for others to surpass, if they dared.

That was 1967, and Gary Wells was barely 10 years old. The Wells family was calling Nevada home at that time so Gary and his dad were at Caesar's Palace. As they stood in the warm Las Vegas night and watched the fantastic leap and the devastating crash that followed, the small, fair-haired kid had a reaction unlike the 20,000 people who watched with him. He wasn't awe-struck by Evel Knievel's courage. He wasn't astounded by the flying figure as it sailed over the spurting fountains. Nor did he wince and moan, trying as the others did to share the pain of Knievel's terrible crash. Instead, young Gary Wells felt only a strong conviction that he too could successfully accomplish the same feat.

To those who knew his reaction, it was perhaps that of a boy dreaming, just a kid who wanted one day to be a cowboy hero, a jet pilot, or a motorcycle jumper. But to Gary himself, who was always quiet and serious, it was no dream. He knew he would someday fly on a motorcycle. Even then, machines were not strange to Gary. Nor was competition. He had been racing go-karts and quarter-midget race cars from the time he was three years old. That's right, three! He loved speed and competition from the moment he first tasted them. And that night at Caesar's Palace, he knew where his future — at least part of it — was heading.

It was still 1967 when Gary began racing motorcycles and for the next four years he devoted himself to the sport. Authorities have called him "a cycling natural." And he proved them right by winning most of the races in which he competed. Gary had one strong advantage to offset his tender age — his father, Ralph Wells, understood his only child's need for cycling and he encouraged him. Together they traveled from Nevada to California, to Arizona, to wherever the competition was best. During those years, Gary won more than his share of motorcross and track cycle races. Racing cycles has been Gary's true love since the day he donned his first helmet. Even today, he talks about returning to racing.

During those four years, most of Gary's time was spent astride a motorcycle, either racing or practicing. He spent long, but enjoyable, hours riding in the desert in Nevada and, later, near Phoenix, Arizona, when his parents moved there. Although he is one of the most proficient cyclists in the world, Gary Wells has never had an operator's license. He's always been too young. So the desert trails where he could ride legally became his second home.

13

There he practiced his jumping form and technique. And there, away from the eyes of others, he prepared himself for the long-range jumping that was to be his destiny.

On August 18, 1971, he made his first public jump at Beeline Dragway in Phoenix. His name was well known to the cycle fans of the area. Shortly after his family settled there, Gary challenged and beat the best cycle racers in Phoenix and earned the number one plate. Beeline Dragway was packed with spectators who came to watch Gary's first jump. He cleared 12 cars with ease, circled the track, and then, to the surprise of everyone, did it again. Two successful jumps — the second measuring 102 feet — wasn't a bad start for a 14-year-old kid with a lot of guts and a cockeyed dream about jumping motorcycles for a living.

Three weeks later, Gary jumped again at Beeline Dragway, this time over 16 cars and the landing ramp. It was an amazing jump for anyone, but for so young a novice, it was unbelievable. The distance and speed were so great that Gary lost control of his bike on landing and crashed with tremendous impact. The rear wheel spokes flew apart like tissue paper and the machine rolled wildly over him as he lay motionless on the ground. He was rushed to the hospital, where he was found to be only slightly hurt — and very lucky. Although his hands were badly skinned, he returned to the dragway to sign autographs and to enjoy the part of his dream that had become a reality.

Like Evel Knievel's fantastic jump at Caesar's Palace, that third public jump at Beeline Dragway was Gary's big moment. The officials said the jump measured a fantastic 155 feet 10 inches — a new outdoor world record! Everyone in Phoenix who saw Gary's jump that night, and many devotees of the sport who did not, declared the skinny young kid the new world record holder. But Evel Knievel, the King of the Stuntmen, had his doubts.

After that, Gary and his father went on tour and Gary jumped in Denver, Colorado; Gary, Indiana; and Marion, Ohio — each time clearing 14 cars with ease. It was during that tour that Gary gained valuable experience both as a cycle jumper and as a performer. Shortly after his fifteenth birthday, Gary had his chance at the big time — the Houston Astrodome. He jumped there successfully on January 15, 1972, over 15 cars. Since then, he has been appearing at fairs and sports events across the country.

Because they are competitors in a big-money business, Evel Knievel and Gary Wells are not very friendly. Gary respects Evel, but resents him. Evel says he welcomes the competition, but doubts Gary's ability. Gary claims the world records, both indoor and outdoor. Evel denies that his own best marks have ever been beaten. And the differences between them do not end with feelings. Evel is 33. Gary is 15. Evel is friendly and outgoing. Gary is shy and quiet. Evel has dark, wavy hair. Gary's is blond, straight, and long. Evel's been jumping publicly for seven years. Gary's been at it barely a year. Evel's been badly hurt many times. Gary's scars are few. It's true that Gary Wells is a "wonder boy." But Evel Knievel is still the "king."

The sport of cycle jumping is young. When Knievel began, he measured his jumps in terms of the number of vehicles he cleared. That was more impressive to the spectators than measurements in footage. Of course, some cars are not as wide as others. Thus, there is disagreement about the existing records. As the sport grows and more and more young men become proficient at it, the American Motorcycle Association will have to establish firm rules to govern it. In the meantime, Gary Wells and young men like him — Super Joe Einhorn and Rex Blackwell, for example — continue to stretch their jumps — to push Knievel, the King, to still greater heights.

2 nd CHAPTER

How It Began

ROBERT CRAIG KNIEVEL was born on October 17, 1938, and grew from infancy to boyhood during the uneasy years of World War II. Butte, Montana, a colorful city in the big country of America's West, was then, as it is now, his hometown. Except for a bigger-than-average share of courage and a wildly mischievous spirit, he wasn't very different from other boys his age. He didn't have wings; he wasn't 10 feet tall; and he always had to put his pants on one leg at a time.

Young Robert's early years were hungry times for the Knievel family. The war made money scarce and prices high. Thus, what he had as a teenager he had to earn.

"My dad never gave me anything," he remembers today, " 'cause we never had anything."

A close look at the picture of R. C. Knievel and one sees a hungry boy from a poor background growing up restless and uncertain in a time when the whole world was also restless and uncertain. Trouble awaited him at every turn, and he was usually there to find it. Most of the juvenile delinquency charges against him in those days weren't serious. He was caught stealing hub caps, fighting, and speeding on the city streets. He was wild and disrespectful of authority, but never was he really an outlaw or criminal as some fables about him suggest. He was just a boy searching for some way to release the pent-up pressure of a troubled boyhood.

It was during that time in his life that he acquired the "Evel" nickname that has stuck with him. He tells just how it happened:

"When I was a kid, I was on a juvenile charge for stealing hub caps in my hometown of Butte, Montana. In the same cell with me, there was a guy named Knauffel who had been indicted on a murder charge for killing a

Chinese woman in a laundry. It came out in the newspaper the next day that the taxpayers had been charged for an extra deputy because 'Awful Knauffel and Evil Knievel' were in jail together and the guard had to be doubled."

He explains that he changed the spelling of his new name because he didn't want it to be like the "necessary evil." And anyway, spelling it "e-v-e-l" made it match the end of his last name. From then on, his given names of Robert and Craig were filed only in the minds of those who knew him as a boy and left to fade on a yellowing birth certificate. Those close to him knew him thereafter as Evel Knievel and it wasn't long before the strange name was echoing about the nation.

When he was 15 years old, he discovered motorcycle racing, a sport that had enough danger, enough excitement, and enough challenge to take the edge off his wild spirit. He quickly became proficient at it, and bested the local competition with ease.

"When I was racing in Great Falls, Montana, as a kid," recalls Knievel, "they would start me in the back row, facing the opposite direction, and I'd still win." And then, with his characteristic egotism, he adds, "I was a terror on wheels!"

Soon the challenge of cycle racing dulled for Evel and he began seeking new challenges.

Anyone could ride a motorcycle on the ground. But no one had dared to fly one farther than the short hop over a fallen tree. The prospect of long-distance jumping, of flying a bike over huge obstacles, fascinated Knievel and he gave much thought to it.

Little is known of his early experiences with cycle jumping. Exactly how he began and how he perfected the art remains his secret. When we speak of courage, we refer to those pioneers who have done what others have not, pioneers like the first man to walk on the Moon or, less seriously, the first man ever to eat a clam. Imagine the feelings of a man speeding for the first time up a ramp to fly a motorcycle over so formidable and dangerous an obstacle as a row of automobiles. Such an act is completely defiant of all the inborn laws of Nature that keep men from killing themselves. In this sense, Evel Knievel is as courageous a pioneer as any in history.

To Knievel flying a motorcycle wasn't the act of an adventurous kid diving from the top of the highest cliff or climbing the tallest tree; it was the exploration of a whole new frontier, a science, a calculated risk. It was the search for an answer to a question he himself had raised: Just how far *could* a man leap on a motorcycle? Since his very first jump, he has devoted his life to finding the answer. And he seeks it yet today.

Each time he bettered his previous jump, the world was sure that Evel Knievel had shown it the best mark a human being could achieve in the strange and dangerous challenge. And each time, the man from Montana returned to the ramps, only to stretch them farther apart, to add more cars to the obstacle, to seek greater marks. So great were his early public jumps that they discouraged others from trying. Who could be proud of swimming across the Hudson River when the English Channel had already been conquered? Who could care about climbing Mt. Whitney after men had stood atop Everest? Who could excite the world with a five-minute mile when another had run it in four? And who could care about a cycle jumper clearing five cars, or six, or even ten, when Evel Knievel was leaping 18 and 19? Indeed, it was his domain for a long time, his "own thing" in an era when doing one's "own thing" was becoming the rule rather than the exception.

There is little doubt that Evel Knievel enjoyed the attention and acclaim that his strange career brought him from the beginning. But it was the money he could earn jumping that led him to abandon all else for his life as a stuntman. As his reputation grew and the demand for him increased, he began earning huge fees for each performance. Thus, cycle jumping gave him the outlet he needed for his restless spirit and the income to escape the poverty into which he'd been born. It satisfied his innermost needs and so he stayed with it. Those who call him crazy could never understand why he jumps.

"Some people tell me I fell on my head at six months and never recovered," says Evel. "But I rather consider myself an explorer, a pioneer in the art of stunt driving and motorcycling."

No, Evel Knievel isn't crazy. Unique, certainly, but not crazy. To understand why he jumps one must know his private feelings. In 1971, after several serious injuries and some great triumphs, he was quoted as saying, "It is better for a person to take a chance from life . . . than to live in that gray twilight and know not victory nor defeat."

And so, in the early years of his career, he built his name and fame with determination, courage, and showmanship. In high school, he'd been a basketball player, a hockey star, and a ski jumper. But motorcycling was his real love and he soon deserted everything else for it. His earliest stunts included a high-speed wheelies and seat stands at 100 miles-per-hour; crashes through flaming walls of fire; leaps over a box of 100 rattlesnakes; and dashes down a landing ramp past two mountain lions tied at the end. He devised glorious stunts that drew large crowds to his performances. And rarely were the crowds disappointed.

In the past seven years, Evel has attempted what has been billed as "The World's Longest Motorcycle Jump" more than 200 times. And he has captured the imagination of the everyday people who have seen his performances; who ride with him in spirit as he leaps through the air; and who, for those brief moments, share his escape from the ordinary. That's why Robert Craig Knievel, the wild kid from the wrong side of the tracks, is the King of the Stuntmen.

3

Evel's Dream; The Canyon Jump

SIX YEARS AGO, while Evel Knievel was building his reputation as a stuntman, he began dreaming of the ultimate jump—a motor-

cycle leap across the Grand Canyon of the Colorado River. When he announced his intention to attempt such a leap, the prospect was met with a variety of reactions. There were those who called him the greatest promoter in the world and saw it as a marvelous rumor to keep the public's interest. Others were more convinced than ever that he wasn't "right" mentally. Some just laughed.

While the public scratched its collective head, Knievel began careful calculations to determine just how he could accomplish the feat. The more he thought about it, the more convinced he became that he could successfully leap a narrow part of the canyon that was approximately one mile in width. As time went on, he made public his intention to actually attempt a canyon jump. More and more people heard of his plan. He received national attention and invaluable publicity. As spectators sat waiting to see him leap over a row of cars, they talked about his plans to jump the Grand Canyon. Many came to see his performances just because they wanted to look at the guy who was going to jump the canyon sometime. Some figured they'd never have the chance to see him afterwards.

In 1966, the Department of the Interior granted Knievel permission for the jump. Immediately, he began working with Harley-Davidson, his major sponsor and America's only motorcycle manufacturer, to design a machine that could meet the demands of such a jump. Suddenly, in 1968, permission was withdrawn by the then Secretary of the Interior Stewart Udall. The stated reasons were that Evel's take-off ramp would be an "eyesore" and that the crowds that came to see him jump would cause irreparable damage to the Canyon's surroundings. It was understandable, since the Grand Canyon *is* one of the seven wonders of the world, a spot on the globe of unequalled natural beauty.

On behalf of Knievel, the famous San Francisco attorney Melvin Belli offered to lease the Canyon from the Navajo Indians and the Bureau of Indian Affairs for the sum of $100,000 so that the stunt could be attempted. Long months of negotiations and legal entanglements followed and eventually the disappointed daredevil was forced to drop the project. But Evel Knievel doesn't quit easily. Actually, he doesn't quit at all.

If he couldn't jump the Grand Canyon, he'd find a canyon he *could* jump, one wide enough and deep enough to provide a spectacular attempt. Soon he found just such a place, the Snake River Canyon near Twin Falls, Idaho. True, it didn't have the promotional appeal of the Grand Canyon nor was it as well known, but it was big and it was spectacular. Although the Snake River Canyon is not quite as deep as the Grand Canyon, it represents an obstacle of three-quarters of a mile in width with a depth of 100 feet. To jump it successfully, Evel figures he'd have to fly just under one mile for a safe landing. And that's about the width he would have faced at the Grand Canyon. The difference in depth doesn't really diminish the danger. The Snake River Canyon is deep enough so that if he missed, if his precautions failed, he would be in as much trouble as with a miss at the Grand Canyon. Put another way, a man can drown as well in eight feet as in 80.

In short order, Knievel leased 300 acres on both sides of the Snake River Canyon for a period of three years. (There are reports, including that of the official Evel Knievel Program, which allege that the daredevil purchased the canyon for the jump. But in a private interview in December of 1971, Knievel informed the author that he had actually leased the property.) He then turned his attentions to perfecting a plan of assault and completing a machine to accomplish it. He also did a bit of promoting, telling the world that his canyon had the highest natural waterfall in the country.

Assured that he wouldn't be blocked in any way from attempting a jump, Knievel began working diligently on a plan.

"I have written permission from the Idaho Land Board," he says. "There's no way they can bring an injunction against me because it's my land. There's no way they can stop me this time."

The suggestion that he will jump almost a mile over an open canyon on a motorcycle sounds impossible at first. But when Knievel explains the details of his plan, the feat begins to sound a bit more plausible. The cycle being built for the canyon attempt is steam-powered and runs on alcohol and special artesian well water. Knievel, the promotor, points out that the water can only be found in the Tumwater River near Olympia, Washington, home of one of his major sponsors, Olympia Beer.

This machine, which Knievel calls an X-2 Sky-cycle, is being built in Anaheim, California, by master mechanic Don Edmunds and will be Harley-Davidson equipped. When completed, it will produce 1800 pounds of thrust and will be capable of accelerating from zero to 350 m.p.h. in eight seconds.

In discussing the jump and the sky-cycle, Evel likes to joke. "Heck, I can jump my Harley — a regular 750cc. motorcycle — a quarter of a mile right now!" Then, laughingly, he adds, " 'Course that's straight down!"

He describes the details of the canyon jump this way: "The take-off ramp for the Snake River Canyon jump will be 300 feet long, 67 feet high, and will have a one-to-one slope. (That means for each foot of elevation, it will extend one foot out.) In addition, there will be a 143-foot runway to the ramp which will give me a total of 443 feet of running surface before take-off. I'll be launched from the ramp

31

at 200 m.p.h. and I will reach between 300 and 350 m.p.h. at the middle of the canyon. The thrust should carry me about a mile. When I'm over solid ground at the other side, I'll deploy my parachute. If it doesn't work and I hit the rock edge of that canyon, I'll probably move the canyon wall back three feet at least! And I'll be embedded in the stone like those presidents in South Dakota!"

Though Evel Knievel is talking about jumping a motorcycle over the Snake River Canyon, it is not to be a cycle jump such as those he has accomplished to date. His sky-cycle is, in the strictest definition, a motorcycle, but it is unlike any in existence today and is closer to a two-wheel jet than a standard bike. And on it, he will not be so much jumping the canyon as flying over it. His landing will be by parachute rather than on a landing ramp. Although these features are essential to a successful conquest of so great a distance, they take his Snake River Canyon jump out of the realm of cycle jumping as we have come to know it today.

Because of a recent injury, the date for the attempt on the canyon has been postponed until July 4 (Independence Day), 1973. Although the King of the Stuntmen expects the largest crowd in athletic history to witness his attempt, he says the big money will come from a documentary motion picture and closed-circuit television.

"I only have one shot at the canyon," he declares, "and I want all the money I can get out of it. A week or so before the jump, I'm going to throw the biggest party in the history of Butte, Montana. I'm going to spend a million bucks in that town. I'll even have to have an armored truck follow me around with the money. That party will have to be held a week or two before the jump so I'll have time to recover from it."

For six years, Evel Knievel has been talking about and planning for his canyon jump. And for six years, people have been excited at the prospect. Some think he'll never actually try it — that it's just a publicity gimmick. Others are certain that someday he'll make an attempt. And if he does, there are those who are sure he'll be killed. Some, devoted Knievel-watchers who believe his slogan, "Color Me Lucky," are sure he'll make it.

Knievel himself only repeats what he has said before, "I just take that bike up there and hope it all works out every time I jump. . . . Hell, I'm the best . . . last of the daredevils . . . and my death will be glorious!"

Whether he attempts a canyon jump in July of 1973, whether he succeeds, or whether he finds his final glory all remain to be seen.

4th CHAPTER

The Glory
and The Agony

EVEL KNIEVEL was 27 years old when he began jumping motorcycles publicly. Today, at 33, he is rich, famous, and horribly scarred. His worst accident came after his most spectacular jump, over the fountains at Caesar's Palace in 1967.

One newspaper report described the performance this way: "It was an incredible act, before 20,000 spectators. See him on the take-off run, his white helmet flashing over the heads of the crowd as he streaks toward the ramp and launches himself into the desert air.

"There he goes, a two-wheeled, metal and flesh birdman from Greek mythology sailing up and up over the white geysers. Impossible! Inconceivable!

"The trajectory peaks. The figure begins the descent. Coming down now, right on the money. For a moment you think he is home free, but the landing fails.

"The motorcycle is cocked a little sideways and it strikes the ramp and compresses, turns, twists, the impact tearing and torturing the metal, popping spokes, then catapulting the white-leathered figure over the bars to slam, bounce, roll, somersault in a dance of disaster for 50 yards with his two-wheeled partner now destroying itself, throwing pieces, wheels, debris."

In the hospital, Knievel learned that the fantastic jump measured 144 feet 6 inches from takeoff to touchdown, the greatest distance ever jumped by a man on a motorcycle. As he received treatment for his injuries — a skull concussion and fractures of the hip, pelvis, and ribs — he talked about his next jump.

"What makes a guy a winner in this business," he said, "is getting out of the hospital and getting up to do it again." Then he added, "If I were starting over, I wouldn't trade any of it for what it's been, good and bad."

When the pain of his crash had subsided, the

usual Evel Knievel humor was heard again. "I figure The Dunes [the resort hotel next door to Caesar's Palace] still owes me 50 bucks for that jump," he declared. "By the time I quit bouncing, I was on their property and I charge at least that much for a personal appearance."

Evel Knievel has had 12 fantastic crashes at performances from Seattle, Washington, to Pocono, Pennsylvania. They've left him with a noticeable limp, more than a hundred broken bones, and what have been called "the most interesting X-rays in the world." Each time he crashed, he dusted himself off, gave his injuries time to heal, and then returned once more to launch his Harley into the air.

"When you crash," he says, "you learn from your mistakes and you don't make the same mistakes again."

It sounds like a painful and risky way to improve, but in cycle jumping, it's the only way. Knievel estimates that he's spent more than $35,000 in hospital bills in the past six years.

No less than 32 insurance companies have refused him insurance, for he is understandably considered a bad risk. Yet, he continues to jump, to take another "chance from life."

In the past six years, Knievel has undergone a dozen open-reduction operations, surgery in which some kind of steel device was put inside him to hold him together. Some say he has so many pins, screws, and plates in him that he clanks when he walks. A pin embedded in his right thigh literally keeps his leg on. And he carries a spare pin with his name engraved on it.

"I have so much metal in me now that I don't get too close to large magnets or junk-yards anymore," laughs Knievel. "Seriously, right now I have too much metal weight, so I'll have to have nine pounds removed from my leg soon. You know, one pound of weight equals a loss of three horsepower on a motor-cycle, and I can't afford that."

A forthcoming operation to remove a steel plate from his leg will take place in Montana as soon as his busy appearance schedule allows.

"I'm going to bring my own private doctor in for this one," says the daredevil, "but I may have to get him a license to practice in Montana. Or maybe he'll have to do it on my kitchen table in the middle of the night. Anyway, we'll get it done."

Some skeptics are doubtful that Evel Knievel has been injured as seriously and as often as he claims. When he's asked how he's able to heal so quickly, he smiles and replies, "I don't know. I think I'm Superman."

Through it all, the King of the Stuntmen has learned what the public finds fascinating about him and his career. It is not only his unbelievable jumps and his constant flirtation with danger, but it's also the crashes and the painful injuries that result from them. There are always those in any crowd watching his performances who have come with a subconscious desire to see him crash. Perhaps they wish him no harm, but they find a special excitement in the disorder of a bad landing. For Evel to jump and land safely is to them an extraordinary feat. But for him to jump, crash, and survive is superb. And the injuries that he suffers from a crash make the danger seem all the more real.

Because of the promotional value he sees in his injuries, Knievel never fails to capitalize on them. If he were to jump, crash, and suffer only a skinned knee, there wouldn't be very much risk in any of it. This isn't to say he hasn't been seriously injured, but there have been times when the extent of his injuries may have been exaggerated. There is no exaggeration, however, in his limp, a painful souvenir of the Caesar's Palace crash, but the gold-tipped cane he carries assures him that the crowds who watch him won't forget it either.

Have his painful crashes made him afraid? Ask him and he'll tell you, "I have no fear! I don't want to get hurt, sure; I'm concerned, but not afraid."

So the man from Montana has come to grips with the dangers of his unique profession. And he's willing to trade the pain of physical injury for the glory of stardom and for the million dollars he hopes to have in the bank by the time he's 40.

At Pocono (Pennsylvania) Raceway, Knievel's appearance was billed as "the last motorcycle performance of the year at the raceway." For him, it was almost his last performance anywhere. He had been in a slump just prior to Pocono and he'd had a couple of misses in preceding weeks that resulted in a few broken bones here and there. In his pre-jump announcement, he discussed the hazards of his profession while clutching his gold-tipped cane. Then he mounted his bike, ran it to test the speed and the tachometer, and was ready.

A reporter for Saga Magazine described the jump this way: "I saw him come shooting up over the ramp. About halfway across the tunnel entrance, everything became quiet. All I heard was the whistling of air, apparently the whistling of a stalled engine . . . he was crossed up . . . How could he come out of it in one piece?

"First the rear wheel . . . landed on the safety ramp and bucked the front wheel hard onto the wooden slats. Knievel couldn't hold onto the handlebars after the terrific jolt and he went flying head first over the front wheel . . .

he went bouncing down the ramp . . . tumbling like a ragdoll."

The terrible wreck left Knievel with a broken sternum, a broken right hand, three broken ribs, and a broken shoulder. He was helped to his feet and walked painfully under his own steam to the start-finish line. The crowd listened in silence as he apologized publicly.

"This business is getting a little too rough for me," he said hoarsely. "I don't know what happened. But a lot of times a guy runs short on nerve."

Everyone there stood and cheered wildly.

Evel's jump at the Houston Astrodome was both sensational and successful. The huge arena stands as a modern-day monument to America's love of sport. The crowd that waited impatiently to see Knievel jump that night was greater in number than any ever attracted to the "Dome" before. Two-day total attendance numbered 85,000. From all walks of life, they came to watch the Montana daredevil who would defy death — or, perhaps, meet it — on a flying motorcycle.

Houston is the home of the nation's astronauts, who are rarely seen publicly in a group. Except for their flights into space, they prefer to travel individually. But when Evel Knievel took his one-man, one-motorcycle show to

Texas, all 19 space explorers and their families turned out to watch the most unique explorer of them all.

Not to disappoint them or the others who'd come to see him jump, the King of the Stuntmen cleared 11 cars and two trucks with ease, accomplishing the jump two nights in succession. Although he says he'd like to return to the Astrodome for another appearance, he doesn't particularly like jumping there because "the place is just too small for a good jump."

At "Cycle-Rama '71" early in that year, Knievel pushed his luck further than ever with a breath-taking leap at the Chicago International Amphitheater. The question there was how fast and how high must a man be traveling on a motorcycle to clear "X" number of cars in an indoor arena with a ceiling just 18 feet high? Careful calculations by the daredevil convinced him that he could sail over 10 autos lined up side-by-side and still have enough headroom to clear the heavy rafters that run across the low ceiling. His figuring proved correct and he completed six successive performances safely. Incidentally, the clearance between his helmet and the rafters on each jump was a scant 12 inches!

When asked if he always calculates that closely, Evel answers, "Yes, and I've been exactly right . . . except for the 12 times I crashed!"

Knievel is proud to report that at the San Francisco Cow Palace he drew a larger crowd than did the Republican National Convention when it was held there in 1964. As usual, he performed spectacularly and the crowd was well satisfied with the show. The fans were even treated to an added Evel Knievel attraction. It seems that a band of Hell's Angels from the notorious outlaw motorcycle gang came to watch one of his performances. During the jump, one of the gang threw a tire iron at the flying daredevil. Evel didn't take kindly to the interference. After he'd finished his jump successfully, he waded into the gang of 12 jeering tough-guys, swinging his gold-tipped cane like an olden-day gladiator. When the smoke cleared, several of his assailants were taken to the hospital for treatment. Although Evel Knievel stands just under six feet and weighs barely 155 pounds, he's a tough man to tangle with.

The Ontario Motor Speedway at Ontario, California, is one of the newest and most elaborate racing facilities in the nation. Because it is located only 40 or so miles from Los Angeles, it has attracted the attention of the Hollywood movie people who find a special fascination in auto racing and the people involved in the sport. Several celebrities, such as Kirk Douglas, Paul Newman, and James Garner, are members of the Board of Directors of the huge speedway. With their flair for the theatrical, the management sought a crowd-pleasing attraction to accompany their February 28, 1971, race, the NASCAR Grand National 500, billed as "the richest stock car race ever held." They picked Evel Knievel to bring in the fans. A crowd of 70,000 people flocked to the speedway to see the show. Many came to watch the stock cars duel for the big pot of gold. But a large part of the crowd was there to witness Knievel's assault on the World Record for motorcycle jumping.

Southern California Dodge dealers furnished 19 Dodge Colts which were lined up side-by-side in the infield. Two hours before the scheduled show time, the crowd began filling the bleachers. Finally, the time came for Evel Knievel's performance. To those who watched, Knievel, the showman, appeared to be caught up in the atmosphere of a movie town crowd. He made countless "speed runs" and "tach runs" to check his machine. He rode toward the take-off ramp and sped past the long line of cars, studying the distance. And it seemed as if he was taking an unusually long time to prepare for the leap. Some in the crowd thought he was "milking" the appearance, as any good showman might. Actually, the extended warm-up was to dissipate condensation in the magneto of Knievel's Harley-Davidson. The machine had been left outside the night before and dampness had collected in the magneto; it had to be dried out before a jump could be attempted.

As the Montana daredevil continued his warm-up near the jump, the crowd tingled with expectation. Dozens of television newsreel cameras rolled; still photographers focused nervously; and three times, the speedway announcer bellowed: "And here he comes!" But each time, at the last second, the XR-750 Harley veered away from the steep take-off ramp.

Finally, he was ready. He gunned the powerful cycle down the approach path, steadying the two-wheeler at 85 miles per hour. Then he climbed the slanted take-off ramp and, in an instant, he was flying straight and true over the longest line of cars ever jumped. Seven seconds of hawklike flight and he landed, a smooth and graceful landing, a display of perfect technique and unequalled skill.

He rolled down the landing ramp effortlessly, but suddenly the crowd sensed that he was in unexpected trouble. The brake chute he uses to cut his speed failed to open. And he was unable to bring the bike to a smooth stop.

Although he slid uncontrollably into a chain-link fence, he was unhurt! Leaving the Harley on its side in the dirt, he walked back to the ramps with his customary limp and his satisfied smile. The crowd went wild!

At the ramps, he called for his bike, which was brought to him, and then he stood and accepted the enthusiastic tribute of the fans for his flawless performance. It was a new world record, with plenty of room to spare. And Evel Knievel deserved the cheers that followed.

There is often an untold story behind what the public sees. At Ontario the day before that record-breaking leap, Knievel lived a drama only a few keen observers realized. As a prelude to the big jump, he attempted to leap over 13 cars — the one-time world record — and cleared them with ease. The performance was an effort to warm up the crowd, to fill the stands for his 19-car attempt the next day. When he hit the take-off ramp for the warm-up jump, the impact jarred the handlebars loose on his Harley. Between the instant they loosened and the moment of flight, the cool daredevil yanked the bars back into place, and thus avoided what could have been a disaster. Instances like that are testimony to his daring and his professionalism. And they explain why he's the "King of the Stuntmen."

No description of Knievel's most outstanding jumps would be complete without mention of his performance at Seattle International Raceway. It was April of 1970, and he had promised a jump over 18 cars, a distance that hadn't been cleared up to that time. A record crowd for that raceway, 14,500 people, came to witness the performance. Before attempting the new record, Knievel announced that he would warm up over 13 cars. With his ramps and the 13-car obstacle set up on the infield grass, he gunned down the approach path and soared over the cars. But he was a hair short! The rear wheel caught the lip of the landing ramp, launching the daredevil and his machine wildly into the air. He hung on in desperation and managed to guide the skidding Harley with its battered rear wheel safely down the ramp to a stop.

Afterwards, Knievel explained, "The rain made the grass wet and the surface too soft to give me the traction I needed. I don't know how I hung on, but I did. The wheel hit just like it did at Caesar's Palace."

But he must have learned from his mistake at that painful crash in Nevada because he managed to avoid similar disaster at Seattle. As his crew moved his ramps to the dry asphalt surface where he could get the necessary traction for the 18-car attempt, he told the crowd,

"This is the first time I've been nervous before a jump."

He was being sincere. After the painful crash at Caesar's Palace, he had vowed that he would never again jump over asphalt. And there he was, in Seattle, facing a line of 18 cars, a distance never before attempted, and it was going to be asphalt all the way. But that's Evel Knievel. He'd promised he would jump 18 cars and, if the grass was too wet, he'd have to do it on asphalt. After all, the crowd had come to see the jump, and the King rarely disappointed his fans. But he had no reason to be nervous. His jump was perfect and another crowd of spectators went home with a new hero.

Knievel's pre-jump announcements have become as exciting a part of his performances as the jumps themselves. Since he ad libs when he addresses an audience, no one knows exactly what he will say. Huge spotlights play on his white-leather jumpsuit with its jeweled cuff links at the sleeves and colorful stars creating a "V" at the neck and a band at the waist. With a microphone in one hand and his ever-present cane in the other, he dominates the scene, capturing the attention of the audience with the same flair as displayed by the world's best showmen.

"I'm glad all of you could make it today,"

he once said. And then he added, "Now I hope I do."

Despite their attitudes when they come to an Evel Knievel performance, most folks are praying for his success once he's made his announcement. He exhibits a measure of sincerity, sprinkled with defiance and concern at the same time — all designed to win the hearts of those who listen.

At the Great Barrington, Massachusetts, State Fairgrounds, Knievel was unable to perform one evening because the steady rainfall had made his ramps too wet to provide him with safe traction. His tests resulted in uncontrollable skidding of the rear wheel. He addressed the crowd:

"Ladies and gentlemen. I have an announcement to make . . . If there is anything that disappoints me, it is to have a little boy or girl boo me. I'm sorry; I apologize. You're a good audience, but I cannot make the jump at this time." Then he added, "If anybody else wants to, they're welcome to try . . ."

There were no takers.

The crowd at Great Barrington was disappointed that night. But the following Saturday, the last night of the fair, Knievel made it up to them. He took the microphone again.

"I'll try my best to make it over the jump

tonight," he said, casually studying the 10-car obstacle.

He made his usual acceleration tests and, when he was ready, he ordered the cover removed from the take-off ramp. (It had been covered in case the rains returned to Massachusetts that night.) Then he roared to the ramp and flew across the spotlights for a perfect landing after a perfect jump. The audience cheered and ran to meet him. There was no disappointment that night.

The list of Evel Knievel's triumphs and tragedies goes on. Wherever he appears, attendance records are smashed as huge crowds come to watch. His is no commonplace performance. Rather, it is a gamble with life that has given him seven years of both glory and agony.

5 th CHAPTER

Evel Sayings

EVEL KNIEVEL has traveled far and wide as an entertainer. Because he is constantly in the public eye and because he has enjoyed so much exposure on television, he has developed an air of sophistication and a glib tongue. At times, he can be moody and quiet. But usually he is "on," and very charming. Without much prodding, he can be coaxed to talk on just about any subject. And he's rarely been guilty of modesty.

"I would say that I am probably one of the most qualified people in the United States to talk about safety," he once told a magazine writer. "About 80 percent of all motorcycle accidents involve cars. And you'll find that out of all the motorcycle-car accidents, the auto driver is at fault some 60 percent of the time." (Evel wasn't far wrong. Statistics indicate that the actual figure is 61 percent.)

Continuing on the subject of motorcycle safety, Knievel says, "The motorcycle rider has to do one thing: He has to wear a helmet when he rides or he's going to be in a lot of trouble. And he has to watch out for automobile drivers, because motorists in the U.S. are not oriented to motorcycles like they are in Europe and Japan. They just don't watch out for them."

And then the world's foremost motorcycle stuntman adds, "A guy is really taking his life in his hands when he gets on a motorcycle and rides on the streets in the United States. I don't ride on the streets myself!"

Although he doesn't think riding a cycle on the nation's streets is a good idea, he offers sound advice for those who wish to learn cycling. "Someone first starting should buy a little motorcycle — like a 100 cc. machine. You don't want to begin with more power than you can handle," advises Knievel. "The motorcycle must be respected ... it's like a jeep; built to do things that an automobile can't do."

He often talks at length on the subject of helmets and helmet law. Once, he said, " ... I might be making a lot of enemies by saying this, but I think there ought to be a law stating that everybody who rides a motorcycle in this country has to wear a helmet. That's the way I think and that's all there is to it. We'd be saving a lot of lives ... and I ought to know."

Does he live by what he preaches? "I'll make a standing offer: If anyone ever sees Evel Knievel on a motorcycle without his helmet on," he says, "I'll give him a thousand dollars cash, right there. And I have some advice for parents who might buy their son a motorcycle for his birthday. Buy him a helmet, too, or you've probably bought him a motorcycle for his last birthday."

Does his thousand-dollar offer apply if he's just, say, coasting down his driveway? To this, he answers, "If the motorcycle is ready to go and I don't have a helmet on, I'll give away a thousand dollars. To be truthful, I just don't get on them without wearing a helmet. And I ride the best motorcycle on the face of the earth ... I bet my life on its reliability."

Knievel is obviously devoted to his major sponsor, Harley-Davidson, and the motorcycles it produces. "I used to crash," he once said, "but that was before I switched to American-made products."

Before his 19-car jump at Ontario Motor Speedway, Knievel announced to the fans, "I've tried to make this jump on a Norton, a Triumph, an American Eagle, and a Honda ... and I've missed it on a Norton, a Triumph, an American Eagle, and a Honda ..."

Then he mounted his Harley XR-750 and proceeded to set a new world's record.

"I've jumped all kinds of motorcycles," says Knievel. "You name it. But I ride a Harley-Davidson. When you bet your life on a bike, it's got to be the best machine available. So I've chosen a Harley 'cause I believe it's the best."

Although his conversation about his cycle sounds like a paid commercial, there is evidence that he has had offers from other manufacturers to use their machines for as much money as Harley is paying him and, sometimes, even more. But he's stayed with Harley.

"My bike is a 750 cc. XR, a limited factory production racing model," he explains. "It is equipped with a parachute system, special seat, and it receives special preparation. My effort is to make the bike as perfect as possible. It weighs 312 pounds soaking wet."

And then with his characteristic flair for exaggeration and braggadocio, he adds, "Why,

I can jump 30 automobiles with the set-up I have now!"

He smiles when he says it, but few listeners doubt him anymore.

Knievel is equally outspoken on the subject of fear. A reporter once asked him, "You have appeared on several television talk shows lately, and many people were surprised to learn that you are apparently so intelligent. If that's so, why do you jump motorcycles?"

To this, Knievel replied, "Because it's easy for me. I can do things a lot of people can't do. There's only one thing that keeps the rest of them from doing what I'm doing: fear."

"And you don't have this fear?" continued the reporter.

"The Grand Canyon doesn't scare me any. The Snake River Canyon doesn't scare me," replied the daredevil. "I may look at a canyon someday that will scare me. But I haven't seen one yet, and I've seen the biggest in the world!"

Obviously, it isn't any fear in himself — at least, not any he'll admit to — that plagues Evel Knievel. But his wife, Linda, has shown that his career frightens her.

"My wife doesn't like my jumping much," says Knievel, "but I do what I want to. You know, it's a woman's fear that stops many a man from being a success."

One subject that brings a quick response

from Knievel is the present crop of young cycle jumpers who have recently stolen some of his spotlight.

"For the past seven years, since my first jump," says the stunt king, with unaccustomed seriousness, "I have had only myself to compete with. I've set and broken all the records. I welcome the competition that's been popping up lately. Why Joe Einhorn was only 14 when I started jumping!"

He begins to get hot under the collar as he continues. "This Gary Wells kid is only 14 or 15 now. I think his whole record thing was a publicity stunt staged by the American Hot Rod Association. . . . I don't think all the guys jumping now could get naked in a barnyard, pour honey on themselves, and attract flies."

After a moment to cool down, the man from Montana adds thoughtfully, "They've sent men to the moon and some have stayed longer and done more, but we'll always remember Neil Armstrong 'cause he was first. It's the same with me!

"I know some day someone may outjump me," he smiles, "but no one will ever out-promote me!"

As far as Knievel is concerned, he still holds the world records.

"My outdoor record is 19 cars plus 45 feet over Dodge Colts. But it was never measured officially," he declares. "My Caesar's Palace jump in Las Vegas was 144 feet 6 inches. My indoor world's record is 133 feet 6 inches over a bunch of vans and Fords. Yes, sir, I still hold the records. Why no one knows how far I can jump. Not even me!"

Considering that Evel Knievel's formal education was limited, his life is, for the most part, a pleasant and rewarding one.

"This is some life," he says. "I enjoy going to work, if that's what it is. Actually, I'm doing what I love to do and, as long as I am, I could go 24 hours a day, seven days a week. I have one pilot and one co-pilot full-time for my private plane and, if they let me, I could wear them out just chauffering me around the sky.

"I've really been on vacation since high school," continues the daredevil, "and I like flying around, drinking beer, riding my cycle, driving my truck, and making eyes at the girls."

Although he has made enough money to afford fancy cars, a nice home, and many of the expensive "toys" of the rich, Knievel's first love is his airplane, a Beachcraft Duke. He lights up when he speaks of it.

"That beauty is a twin-engined turbo-charged job, good for 200 miles per hour on the ground. But we were doing 350 the other day at take-off . . ."

"Yeah, but that was with strong tail winds,"

adds his pilot, Denny Davis, dulling the exaggeration.

Despite his apparent bravado, there have been some rumors that Evel is afraid of flying.

"I never have liked flying," he once said, "but I took it up after my first 100,000 miles in the air on commercial airliners. What scares people is the unknown. I always want to know what's going on. Once you get up front and find out what's happening, you understand where your life is — not just in somebody else's hands.

"The other day, I was at the controls of the Duke while Denny was in the back of the plane," he continued, "and there was so much air traffic that I was shaking like a leaf."

Someday he hopes to find the time to really learn to fly and to earn his license.

"I'd like to go to the moon," he's often said, "but only as the command pilot!"

If he's serious, he's going to have to do a lot more flying than he's done on either his motorcycle or in his plane.

He sees an additional benefit in flying. "I think flying will help me with my canyon jump," he says. "Although it will only be a few seconds of actual flight, a knowledge of aviation could help. I'm even thinking of putting a gyroscope on my sky-cycle."

When Evel Knievel talks about his family,

the swaggering, defiant showman suddenly becomes a warm, sincere husband and father. He and his wife, Linda, have three children: Kelly, 11; Robby, 9; and Tracey, 7.

"I'd like my boys to jump," he says, " 'cause it's been a good life for me. But right now they like Little League baseball and school too much to be serious about it.

"You know, my kids all ride horses and cycles already," he continues proudly. "They like my jumping. One good thing about my business: It's given me the opportunity to take my kids all over the country. They've been to the top of the Empire State Building . . . Arlington Cemetery in Washington . . . all over. And they've met all kinds of celebrities. It's all been really educational for them, and for me too."

Money was one of the main reasons why Evel Knievel pursued the risky profession of a cycle jumper. Yet, he has very little respect for it.

". . . I read in a Los Angeles newspaper that I was the highest paid athlete in the world," he said in 1971, "but this year, I will be third, because Clay and Frazier would be first and second. I don't know how much money I make . . . I'm always broke. I made $750,000 last year. But I spent it all too!"

On the subject of finances, he told one reporter, "I don't believe in saving money. I believe in spending it. Oh, I've put a few bucks away for my kids, but I believe no kid should get anything — education included — for nothing; without working for it. You have to want to work for something. That way, a kid will be working too hard to get in trouble."

That advice is from a guy who's been in and out of trouble all his life.

Of necessity, Knievel has become not only an outstanding showman, but a cautious businessman. After all, he *is* big business. Rumor has it that he receives $100,000 annually from his two largest sponsors, Harley-Davidson Motorcycles and Olympia Beer. In addition to that, he commands a minimum appearance fee from a promoter of $25,000. But he doesn't like dealing with promoters. He's been "clipped," as he says, too often in the past.

"I'd rather deal with track owners who have a place of their own than with promoters. You know, a promoter is like a guy walking around with two pieces of plain bread just looking to find a piece of cheese.

"When I deal with a raceway manager like, say, Bob Huff of Tucson, I get a percentage of the gate. I try to work with them. Heck, if I don't get $5,000 a month, I can't even live . . . But when I deal with a promoter, he's gotta guarantee me $25,000 or it's no show."

Bob Huff, manager of Tucson Dragway in Tucson, Arizona, also enjoys dealing with Knievel. "He's the only guy to ever block Speedway Boulevard in Tucson," says Huff. "The fans love him. And I find him more than fair to deal with."

What does the future hold for Evel Knievel?

"I'd like to complete my canyon jump," he responds, "and then accept some of the offers I've received to appear in Europe and Japan. Then I'd retire. You know, I'm in the land and heavy equipment business also. I'd just play golf then, and learn to fly . . ."

Then he smiles and adds, "Lately, I've been reading about so many guys outjumping me, that I've been thinking about quitting just so's I can have time to go watch them!"

But he won't quit, not for a while yet. There are still too many unconquered obstacles; too many people who haven't seen the bottom of his wheels as he flies through the air; too many dollars to be made; and too many moments of glory still waiting for him.

"You know, I'd like to write a book of my own one of these days," he once said, "just to tell what the movie about me couldn't — to expose all the promoters who are cheating the public."

6th CHAPTER

The Motion Picture: "Evel Knievel"

IT WAS DECEMBER OF 1971 — just a week before Christmas — and Evel Knievel had

flown to Tucson, Arizona, from his home in Butte to plan a future appearance in the sprawling desert city. With him as he sat in the restaurant of the lavish Aztec Inn were his pilot and co-pilot, an assistant, and a couple of reporters. After the usual conversation about his career, the reporters began questioning him about the recent motion picture of his life.

"The movie they did about me," he replied when asked, "was about 90% true. Of course, there was some exaggeration, but you know how Hollywood is. And they had to leave a lot of stuff out too!" He smiled widely.

"You did the actual jumping and the stunts for the film, didn't you?" asked one reporter.

"Who else could have done 'em?" retorted Knievel, grinning.

"How come you didn't play the lead role yourself?" continued the interviewer.

"You know, life goes by like that," answered Knievel, snapping his fingers, "no matter how long you live. And I don't want to pretend I'm somebody else, even if it's a movie version of me. I'd rather be doing something." Then very thoughtfully, he added, "No, I didn't want to act in it. I'm no actor! I'm a con man. But you know something. When that rear wheel leaves the takeoff ramp, the con is gone!"

Although his public attitude toward the film has often appeared flip in the press and on television, those close to Knievel claim that he was secretly thrilled that the film was made.

Actually, the picture was the brain-child of its star, veteran actor George Hamilton, who may be better remembered by non-moviegoers as the fellow who once dated President Lyndon Johnson's daughter Lynda.

Here are excerpts from an article in the

July, 1971, edition of "The Motorcycle Enthusiast In Action," a Harley-Davidson newsletter, discussing the film:

"Now, appearing soon at theaters all over the country, is the as-it-happened true story of Evel Knievel. The Fanfare Corporation production 'Evel Knievel' stars veteran actor George Hamilton in the title role with 'Lolita' star Sue Lyon as Linda Knievel. Co-starring is a Harley-Davidson XR 750 as the bike which carries Knievel to a new world record long distance motorcycle jump.

"The film was shot on location in Butte where Evel grew up and in Los Angeles. It traces his life from his untamed youth in Montana where he experienced scrapes with the law to his present occupation as daredevil stuntman where he brushes shoulders with death itself . . ."

During the shooting of the film in Butte, Knievel joined the movie company to serve as advisor on the picture. The local folk were quite excited about the arrival of a Hollywood motion picture company in their city and many of them agreed with very little persuasion to act as "extras."

Knievel himself also appears briefly in the film. Although the star, George Hamilton, taught himself to master the motorcycle for the role, it's the real Evel doing the jumping.

Hamilton, however, does perform one stunt — his first for the camera in his long acting career. The footage of Evel includes his world record jump over 19 cars at Ontario Motor Speedway.

Evel Knievel and George Hamilton met long before anyone suggested a movie of the stunt-man's life. Because of the friendship that developed between them, Hamilton purchased the rights to Evel's life story and proposed to produce a film in conjunction with the Fanfare Film Corporation. MGM studios were used for the Hollywood footage. The remainder of the film was shot on location where the events actually happened.

Movie critics applauded the film and Hamilton's performance, claiming that his portrayal is superb "right down to Evel's slight limp, the proud tilt of his head, and the self-assured mannerisms."

Following are some excerpts from the screen play.

In the film, Knievel makes his first public jump at a Montana rodeo. Here is his speech to the audience prior to that jump.

Bobby Knievel, ladies and gentlemen, and I'm sure proud to be here with you. It's an honor to know so many nice folks want to take time out from all the other things they got to do to come and see me jump these cars. Now I want you to know that motorcycling's getting itself a bad name these days, a real bad name, and you take a look at all them weirdos riding around on their fancy bikes, you gotta know the reason for that. Well, I'm here to tell you that they don't mean a thing, ladies and gentlemen. They just giving the motorcycle a bad name, and I'm here today, in front of all you nice folks, to show you that there's more to motorcycling than beating up on little old ladies and scaring the . . . the heck outa everybody gets in their way. All of them medals and things they tie around their necks, it don't mean a thing, and I'm here to show you what a motorcycle can really do if you know how to ride it. I'm sure proud to be here, and I thank you ladies and gentlemen.

STAGE DIRECTIONS: "He moves off down the ramp, acknowledging the applause, revelling in it. He mounts his bike, drives to the base of the ramp, wheels around, rides into position for the jump, and pauses, milking it. Even now there is a certain amount of braggadocio, but not as much as we'll see later on. The CAMERA takes time to study his face; it's a new excitement for him, and though he doesn't yet know it, it's the beginning of a whole new career. . . ."

In a later scene, Evel prepares to jump again and makes his announcement to the audience. It is much later in his career and he has become a polished professional.

It is my honor and privilege to show you the most spectacular motorcycle jump in the entire history of dare-deviltry. That's right and that goes back a long way. Now a lot of folks have been saying that what I am trying is not possible and

there was one guy who said that I just didn't
know when to be scared. That I did not know
when to quit. Well, that fellow was right. I don't
know when to quit and I hope to the good Lord
that I never find out. And that man was right
when he said that I didn't know when to be
scared. I don't know because the word fear does
not exist in my vocabulary. No it doesn't. When I
want to do something that oughta scare the living
daylights out of me, I don't sit around and worry
about it. Teddy Roosevelt, the greatest president
this country ever had, said that it is a weak man
who fears what will arise out of the consequences
of his actions — a strong man fears only God, and
that's what I live by. And I got a message for all
you fine young people and I see a lot of 'em out
there today. My message is that when you want
to do something, just take those bars in your
hands, turn that throttle and do it . . .

STAGE DIRECTIONS: "Foot hits gear — wheel
spins — exhaust fires flame — cycle exits . . ."
In the film, Evel crashed badly in the jump
following that speech.

In a later scene, he runs out of the hospital
after a bad wreck. In the parking lot, he
mounts his motorcycle as doctors and nurses
try to stop him. They've told him he'll never
walk again.

. . . Never walk again . . . hell, I'm riding already.
They approach warily.

I do what I'm best at. There is no second best at
stunt motorcycling — none at all. There is no one

in the entire field of dare-deviltry that has my
style or conviction.

More doctors rush out, attendants, nurses also.
They all stop some distance from him, afraid
to come closer.

When I was a kid in high school, my football
coach said: "Knievel, you don't have any team
spirit and this school was founded on the idea of
the group — everyone pulling his weight. You
don't understand that and that's why you'll never
make the team . . .

They are getting closer.

I said, what do you mean, team? I don't need no
team to back me up.

They are almost upon him. He accelerates,
loses control, and crashes. They all rush over.

In the final scene of the film, Evel rides
alone beside a huge canyon, with his voice
heard in the background.

Important people in this country, celebrities like
myself, Elvis, Frank Sinatra, John Wayne, we
have a responsibility. There are millions of people
that look at our lives and it gives theirs some
meaning. I don't understand this but that's the
way it is. People come out from their jobs —
most of which are meaningless to them and they
watch me jump 20 cars — maybe get splattered —
it means something to them. They jump right
alongside of me, they take the bars in their hands
and for a split second — they're all daredevils. It
means something — I am the last gladiator, the
only gladiator in the new Rome. I go into the
arena and I compete against destruction and I win
and next week I go out there and do it again.

In this time, civilization being what it is and all, we have very little choice about our life. The only thing really left us is a choice about our death — and mine will be . . . glorious."

Although much of the film suffers from the Hollywood influence, it captures much of Knievel, the King.

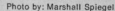

(*Photo right*) *Evel Knievel brings his Harley down for a soft landing; (below) Knievel, left, and the author share a light moment after a 1971 interview in Tucson, Arizona.*

Photo by: Marshall Spiegel

(Photo right) Film stars George Hamilton and Sue Lyon as they portrayed Mr. and Mrs. Knievel in the motion picture, "Evel Knievel." (below) Knievel's $140,000-tractor-trailer.

(Photo above) The master showman addresses his audience before a jump; (above right) Knievel pays careful attention to his machine; (right) and he never mounts it without donning his helmet.

Evel Knievel, the King, and the Harley-Davidson that made him Number 1.

7th CHAPTER

The King's Machines

THE MONTANA DAREDEVIL loves machines — especially motor vehicles — and well he should since they have made him famous. He's jumped his motorcycles over cars, trucks, tractors, and vans. And with the money he

earned, he's bought motorcycles, cars, trucks, tractors, vans, airplanes . . .

His personal motorized caravan includes a '71 Caddy station wagon. Of it, he says, "There are only three in existence — mine, Dean Martin's, and Keith Allen's. He's the boss of the Philadelphia Flyers. Mine's the only '71. Cost me $23,000, but I added a special $3,000 paint job."

To carry the tons of ramps and equipment he needs to perform, Knievel has a specially-built $140,000 tractor-trailer, custom-constructed by Kenworth of Kansas City, Missouri. The cab-over diesel tractor has a 14-speed Allison automatic transmission and it houses his office, dressing room, and lounge. It is tastefully decorated both inside and out, and is equipped with color television, stereo, air-conditioning, and a thermostatically-controlled heating system. The trailer is fitted to carry the eight tons of takeoff and landing ramps; several motorcycles, including the jet-bikes being prepared for his assault on the Snake River Canyon; and his custom Ford Ranchero pick-up. The Evel Knievel tractor-trailer, like its owner, has distinction. It is the longest vehicle of its kind in the world, according to the daredevil's publicity people.

In addition to a fleet of grocery-getters, a variety of cars that Linda Knievel uses back in Butte, Evel is also the proud owner of a magnificent Rolls Royce, one of his few machines that he pampers.

The machine responsible for all his wealth and success is the Harley-Davidson XR-750. Although Knievel's bikes, those he uses for his jumps, are specially equipped and prepared, they begin from stock machines. Here are the features and specifications of a stock XR-750:

FEATURES:

1. 750 cc. O.H.V. engine with tuned exhaust pipes; Fairbanks-Morse Magneto; Tillotson racing carburetor; 4-speed transmission; and aluminum pushrods.
2. Welded High Boy tube frame; 4130 material with swing arm rear suspension.
3. Lightweight fiberglass seat-fender with foam cushion.
4. Lightweight fiberglass gas tank with 2½ gallon capacity.
5. Ceriani racing front fork with aluminum fork bracket.
6. Girling racing rear shock absorbers.
7. 19-inch aluminum wheels and rims, front and rear.
   Front tire — 4.00 X 19 Pirelli Universal
   Rear tire — 4.00 X 19 Goodyear All-Traction
8. Aluminum oil tank with three quart capacity.
9. Aluminum ball end clutch lever.
10. ⅞-inch diameter handlebars; quarter-turn spring return throttle control; and large diameter rubber hand grips.

SPECIFICATIONS:

ENGINE — 45 cubic inches; 748 cc. overhead valve; twin cylinder. Bore 3.005 inches. Stroke 3.219 inches. Compression ratio 9.5 to 1.

TRANSMISSION — Standard ratio.

PRIMARY DRIVE — 25-tooth motor sprocket; 59-tooth clutch; triple-row roller chain.

REAR DRIVE — 16-tooth transmission sprocket; 40-tooth rear wheel sprocket; overall drive ratio 5.90 to 1.

COLOR — Jet Fire Orange.

Exactly what Evel Knievel and his mechanics

do to a stock XR-750 to make it a "flying machine" is unknown. However, aside from a few well-kept tricks of the cycle-jumping trade, and special paint, his bikes are practically stock. One thing's for sure, though: Not everyone can buy an XR-750 Harley and go cycle jumping; at least, not like the King of the Stuntmen. There's no doubt that a good machine makes it possible. But there's much more to it than that.

The specifications for Knievel's Sky-Cycle, the machine he'll use for his canyon jump, and another "trick" bike he's had built are well-guarded secrets. The Sky-Cycle, which is also known as the X-2, will be capable of 350 miles per hour and will be steam powered. His X-1, also a Harley-Davidson equipped machine, is capable of 200 m.p.h. He hasn't said what he'll do with that one yet, but it could be for leaping the 25 cars he plans to conquer before he hangs up his helmet. Or perhaps he'll use it for hopping over small canyons.

One of the problems he is still facing is selecting a tire for his Snake River Canyon jump on July 4, 1973.

"I haven't chosen a tire yet," he said early in 1972, "but I'm looking at Firestone, Goodyear, and a European make. When I do choose one, you can bet it will be the best and safest tire for the job in the world. I'm testing now.

Actually, going up the ramp at the speed I'll be traveling will be a tough job for any tire."

Obviously, the promotional value of a successful canyon jump by Evel Knievel would be priceless to any tire manufacturer. It's a safe guess that he'll select a tire that will do the job, but it will also be made by a manufacturer willing to pay a large price for the exposure. That's how Evel Knievel operates. And no one can blame him for wanting to squeeze every dollar out of his career. After all, it could end almost anytime.

8th CHAPTER

Hail The King!

"YOU KNOW, I've heard guys talk and exaggerate about me and what I've done," said Evel Knievel once to a reporter. "Some of them have me jumping clean over the state of Arizona! But they do that 'cause they really believe it . . ."

True, Evel Knievel is an egotist, but he's

also sensitive and usually likable. He rarely
minces words and he never polishes apples.
He's the King of the Stuntmen and, if the
world wants to witness his special talent, it
may do so only on his terms. His life is hectic
and disorderly. And he seldom knows where
he's heading next.

85

". . . I don't ever book ahead," he once said, " 'cause you just can't do that in my business. You see, there is such a word as 'can't' when you're jumping motorcycles. I'm not an insurance salesman who bluffs himself into believing what he can do the next day.

"I sold insurance one time," he rambled. "I think I sold 110 policies in a single day and 271 in a week. I used to get up in the morning, beat myself on the chest, and say, 'I can do anything!' And if I couldn't, I used to believe that in every adversity there is an equivalency in good fortune. . . . If you look for it hard enough, you can find it.

"But that's not the way it is in real life. If men like Peale, Carnegie, W. Clement Stone, and Napoleon Hill, who wrote many good books — 'The Power of Positive Thinking' and so on — were to write a book entitled 'There Is No Such Word As Can't,' and they got on motorcycles and tried to jump 19 cars and only made 18, they'd pick themselves up and say, 'Man, I can't do that. I can't make it.'"

From conversation like that, it becomes apparent that the defiant, cocky daredevil from Montana is not only well read, but can also be articulate.

Yes, Evel Knievel knows that there are some obstacles that just can't be conquered. Ask him if he'll succeed prior to a jump he's never tried, and he'll answer, "I think I'll make it. If I don't, I'm man enough to take care of the consequences."

How long will he continue to jump? Some of his followers think he'll quit after the canyon jump, when and if he finally attempts it. Others are certain that the canyon jump will finish him for good. He himself says he'll go on jumping as long as his motorcycle is "talking good" to him. One thing's for sure, when he finally does retire, it will take a long time and a lot of spectacular leaps before anyone can claim the King's crown. The world of stunts and stuntmen belongs to Evel Knievel. And his name will long be remembered by those of us who admire that special brand of insane courage that makes men like him do what they do.

Being top dog isn't always easy. Knievel knows that. And he knows also that he must continue to be more spectacular, more daring, and more colorful than those who dare to copy him. As he says, "I've got to be the best at what I do!" But he is no longer alone in the world of cycle jumping. As time goes on, it will be exceedingly more difficult for him to remain the best. Yet, he doesn't believe that the competition has developed enough to pose a threat to him at the present time.

"I'm a God-fearing man," he said a while

back, "but I don't believe most of this do-gooder stuff. With all the guys jumping now who are supposed to be outjumping me, I don't believe anything anymore. I just cancelled my subscription to my local paper 'cause of that."

Knievel is skeptical about any cycle jumping accomplishments, except, of course, his own. And he refuses to acknowledge the presence of anyone else in his domain.

"This kid, Gary Wells, never jumped no 156 feet like they claim," says the daredevil convincingly. "He had part of his cars under a safety ramp. It was all a big phoney, a big publicity thing. He has a 54-foot landing ramp and 15 cars with four or five cars covered by a safety ramp — the cars are about six feet wide when set — that's not nearly 156 feet . . . I never even use a safety ramp.

"Look, I'm not ashamed to get beat by a great rider or jumper," he adds, "but not by this phony stuff . . . "

It sounds like an easy problem to solve. If the heavyweight champion of the world wants to prove that he's better than a contender, all he need do is meet him in the same ring. Why then doesn't Evel Knievel jump off against Gary Wells? He says he will — anytime and any place. But there's one catch: Money!

"They're paying the kid $1,500 to jump at

the Astrodome," said Evel prior to Gary's appearance in Houston. "I'll put up $100,000 that no one can outjump me. I'll go against him — against anybody — for $125,000 appearance money . . . and I'll go."

It's understandable that Knievel demands a large amount of money for a jump-off against Gary Wells or any other young challenger. Such an appearance would be risky business for him. He could be seriously injured, but that's a chance he takes every time he mounts his cycle. Even worse, he could lose. He tells the world it could never happen, but in his heart he knows it's possible. It would be very expensive for the King to be dethroned publicly—undisputably whipped before the world — by some kid.

Late in the summer of 1971, Harley-Davidson issued a press release on behalf of their favorite son. It read in part:

"Recent and inaccurate claims by amateur motorcycle jumpers have prompted a response from World's Record Jumper Evel Knievel, who has requested that news media be informed correctly of his existing records. . . .

"Effective immediately Evel Knievel announces a wager, to any challenger, for a cash total of $25,000 for any match jump. The conditions of the wager are: a challenger must put up equal money; (b) challenger to use his own motorcycle; (c) no safety ramps will be used; (d) jump distance to be measured and verified by state or local or A.M.A. (American Motorcycle Association) officials not affiliated with either jumper or any of their sponsors or promoters."

There haven't been any takers to date. Offers have been made. And promoters have tried to arrange a match jump between Evel and Gary Wells. But the King has his price and it's a lot of money. No one can really blame him for the conditions he demands. After all, he's still in the driver's seat. But the day may come when cycle-jumping competition and match jumps will be the only way one can earn the number one jumping plate and the title of King.

"I'm proud that these guys are jumping . . . kids like Gary Wells," said Knievel last Christmas. "Why he was only, what, eight or nine years old when I started and he wanted to do what I did. My dad tried to stop me from riding a cycle. But Gary's father encouraged him. . . ."

His face grew very serious as he continued, "The kid's father is 'the Flying Yarnman' and he's in a big hurry. Know what? The kid's gonna get hurt. Like Joe Einhorn did the other night at the Cow Palace in Frisco. He was short of my indoor record and crashed into the wall. He's in the hospital with a real bad brain concussion . . ."

Then with characteristic Knievel egotism, he added, "But he'll be all right. I sent him a telegram wishing him well."

Whether Evel Knievel is truly worried about the competition is difficult to tell. It's a safe guess that he cannot completely ignore the threat of the young lions like Gary Wells. But Knievel is a tough man to scare, obviously. It looks as though he'll continue to leap his Harley through the air over larger and larger obstacles; to talk and dream about his canyon jump; and to reap as much fame and wealth as he can from both. He's earned the right to call the shots. After all, he started the whole thing. And he *is* still the King.

9th CHAPTER

Who's this kid Gary Wells?

ON WEDNESDAY, AUGUST 18, 1971, an unusually large crowd of spectators filled Bee-

line Dragway in Phoenix, Arizona. As the program began, all eyes focused on a slender, young kid with straight blonde hair and a baby face. To the motorcycle fans of Phoenix, this kid, Gary Wells, was no stranger. Since his family moved there from Nevada a year or so earlier, they'd heard about him and watched him. And they'd seen the fourteen-year-old newcomer trounce the local cycle racing competition unmercifully. Within three months

after the Wells family — Gary; his father Ralph; and his mother Hazel — settled in Phoenix, Gary had beaten all the two-wheeled racers in the area, including the 15-year racing veteran, Byron Boaz. For the preceding 10 years, Boaz had dominated the sport in Phoenix. Although Boaz is a superb cyclist who gained his status in tough competition, he was unable to keep the number one license plate once young Gary Wells set out to win it from him. Shortly thereafter, Wells also received the sponsorship of a local cycle shop, support that had previously belonged to Boaz. The cycle fans of Phoenix who jammed Beeline Dragway that night had come to know Gary Wells and to applaud his uncanny riding ability.

But the kid's appearance that hot August evening was not for a mere motorcycle race. The publicity said that he was going to jump his motorcycle over some cars — 12 to be exact! It was his first public appearance as a cycle jumper and it promised to be interesting, if not exciting. There were those in the crowd who thought the kid was trying to copy Evel Knievel. Others thought it was a gag — that the kid wouldn't really try it. Some figured that, if he did, he'd wipe out. But there were also those, like his father, who not only knew he'd make it, but were sure he'd do it with style.

As Gary carefully checked his Montesa and prepared for his attempt, he too wondered how it was going to go. In practice, the jump had been "a piece of cake." But now he was concerned about the crowd that had come to watch. He knew there were those who'd like to see him fail.

"It wasn't easy for me when my family first moved to Phoenix," remembers Gary. "The local guys were after me, but I never worried about them. I just raced to win ... even though there were a couple of guys who threatened to put me into the concrete wall."

To the fans high in the bleachers, the skinny kid didn't look much like a stuntman or a performer. Those who had seen an Evel Knievel appearance noted the differences immediately. Nowhere was the fanfare of a professional entertainer. Nowhere were there fancy takeoff and landing ramps. Or a gleaming white leather suit. Or a specially-painted motorcycle. No, the kid looked ordinary. His ramps were plain and unsightly. His leathers were common and well worn from many miles of motocross and cycle racing. And his bike was just a run-of-the-mill Montesa with no special charm. But the kid was there to jump 12 cars and he figured that, even without the frills, what he had could get the job done.

At 8:35 p.m., just five minutes after the

announced time, Gary fired up his machine and the staccato roar of its engine filled the night air. Lacking the experience of a seasoned performer, the kid didn't bother to charge up the crowd with a spectacular warm-up. He gunned his bike up and down a few times to check its speed and tachometer. And he headed full tilt to the steep takeoff ramp. True, from the stands, everything about the kid and his performance looked ordinary — everything, that is, but the way he sailed over those 12 cars. His form and technique were flawless both on takeoff and landing. And his flight through the air was graceful and breathtaking. The crowd shouted and clapped its appreciation! But before the echo of that roar had stopped, the kid was on his way back up the takeoff ramp. The crowd sat silent and wide-eyed as the kid once again soared above the 12-car obstacle for a second perfect jump and landing. It was like a televised instant re-play, a second chance to see what unbelieving eyes had recorded only moments before. Fourteen-year-old Gary Wells had successfully accomplished what only a handful of men of any age had ever tried. And he'd done it twice! Who said the kid wasn't a showman?

"I jumped the same jump twice that night," says Gary. "Once to show them I could do what Evel Knievel did, and the second time, just to show them that I could do it twice!"

The angle of Gary's takeoff ramp had sent him 50 feet high in the air. His second jump measured 102 feet exactly. Not only had he cleared the 12 American Motors Gremlins which are each approximately\six feet wide, but he had landed several feet farther down the landing ramp than was anticipated. His take-off speed was close to 65 miles per hour, a bit too fast for that distance. But it was better to jump long in his first appearance. Experience would teach him what he needed to know about gauging his takeoff speed.

Early the next morning, the world of cycle jumping was informed that the kid from Phoenix, Gary Wells, had become the second man to jump such a distance. Only Evel Knievel, the King of the Stuntmen, had jumped farther. Newspaper reports on Gary's performance mentioned that the Gremlins, furnished by Randall American in Mesa, Arizona, had been chosen because they are the widest cars in their class — almost a foot wider than the Dodge Colts used by Evel Knievel in his record-setting jumps. Such publicity coupled with statements made by Gary and his father after the jump clearly indicated that they were planning to challenge King Knievel for his world-record title.

Cycle-jumping devotees had mixed reactions. Sure, the kid had cleared 12 cars in a dusty dragway somewhere out in the desert of Arizona. But he was a beginner and it could have been beginner's luck. It had been the very first special event in the history of Beeline Dragway, and maybe the track owners, the spectators, and the newspaper reporters were exaggerating the kid's form and technique. Maybe they were even exaggerating the distance. Then again, the reports said the kid had cleared the jump twice in the same night. Perhaps there were skeptics among those who heard of Gary's first performance. But it wasn't long before all of cycledom — skeptic or not — was asking, "Who's this kid Gary Wells?"

They didn't have to wait more than 18 days for an answer. On Sunday, September 5, Gary Wells returned to jump again at Beeline Dragway. The crowd was even bigger this time. Drawn by the publicity of his previous appearance and freer to attend a Sunday performance, the fans flocked to the dragway. This time, the kid would attempt to clear 16 cars, a distance close to the existing outdoor world record. And this time, the curious who knew nothing of cycling joined the enthusiasts to watch Gary jump.

The night was clear and the desert breezes gentle. As Gary fired his Montesa, he noticed that the two American flags on his landing

ramp hung lifeless. This meant that there
wasn't enough wind to bother him. He'd
learned that a stiff breeze could be disastrous
if he tried jumping into it. No, conditions
were perfect.

He had made two mistakes during his first
appearance: He'd failed to warm up the crowd
and he'd overestimated his takeoff speed. In
this second performance, he was destined to
correct one, and repeat the other. Prior to his
actual jump, he treated the crowd to a series
of "wheelies," in which he rode straight and
steady on just the rear wheel. Then he earned
their applause by doing a one-hand version
while offering the "peace sign" with his free
hand. This maneuver has become his trade-
mark since. He also rode his Montesa back-
wards to the cheers of the fans. Then he ran
to check his speed and tachometer. And ran
again to be certain it was right. He approached
the takeoff ramp once and veered away from
it as the crowd gasped. And then he did it!
His bike roared up the ramp at 95 miles per
hour and he soared into the air as though he
would never come down. He was still high in
the air as he passed over the sixteenth car. And
the rubber of his tires never did touch the
wood of his landing ramp as he came down
several feet beyond it. But the terrific thrust
of the jump and the shocking impact of the

landing made it impossible for him to keep his balance. Suddenly he crashed and tumbled violently!

The crowd shrieked and then there was silence. The Montesa's engine sputtered on as the bike came to rest, fallen on its side with its front spokes smashed and its wheels and rear axle bent like discarded toys. The impact had been so great that it twisted the solid steel foot peg on the right side. Several feet away, the kid lay motionless, his thin form twisted in a way God never intended the human body to twist.

It was a full five minutes before Gary Wells stirred. When he did, he showed the stuff of which all cycle jumpers must be made as he walked to the ambulance under his own steam. Meanwhile, a mad scramble to measure the actual distance of his jump was taking place. A group of officials, including movie-star and motorcycle-buff Keenan Wynn, and Gary's father, Ralph, stretched a measuring tape and announced an unbelievable distance — 155 feet 10 inches!

As the shrill siren of the ambulance signaled Gary's removal to the hospital, the crowd sat in disbelief, each person mentally calculating the phenomenal distance that had been announced over the loudspeaker. *A jump of 155 feet 10 inches! Why that's equivalent to*

26 Gremlins or 31 Dodge Colts! That's 60 feet 10 inches farther than Knievel's world record! Then someone shouted, "Hey, that kid just set a new world's record!"

Before the excitement of the crowd had dissipated, Gary was back from the hospital. The fantastic crash had left him with only minor injuries — badly scraped hands and wrists — and a few aches and pains. He forgot the injuries as he signed autographs and graciously accepted the admiration of his fans, many of whom had joined the fold that very night.

"I didn't plan going that far," said Gary when he and his father finally found the time to analyze what had happened. "I guess my takeoff speed of 95 was a bit too fast."

Actually, the jump had been calculated for 107 feet with a takeoff speed of 90. But a five-mile-per-hour error can be far too much in cycle jumping. The newspapers reported that he had jumped a full 10 feet beyond the landing ramp. But some witnesses weren't sure exactly where he landed. Everyone agreed that his landing form had been good, and that he probably wouldn't have gone down if the front forks on his Montesa hadn't given way from the tremendous impact of the landing. Whatever happened, the kid had given the world one fantastic jump!

That performance, on September 8, 1971 —

his second public appearance and only his third public jump — served notice to the world that Gary Wells had entered the big league of motorcycle jumping. Since then, few have asked, "Who's this kid Gary Wells?" They know.

Gary Wells and one of his many fans. The photo on pages 92 and 93 shows how he got to claim the record. Photo by: Marshall Spiegel

10th CHAPTER

The Making of a Cycle Jumper

HOW DOES AN AVERAGE BOY develop into a professional cycle jumper by the age of 14? The story of Gary Wells is the only real answer to that question. He was born Ralph Gary Wells, Jr., on November 21, 1956, to Ralph and Hazel Wells, then of Seattle, Washington. From the moment Ralph Wells first studied the fair-haired infant, he knew his son — his only child —would someday be "somebody" in motor competition. He just knew it. It's true that Gary Wells drew his first breath as an average boy, but his father had a burning determination that he be more.

Ralph Wells had never been a great success at anything he undertook. But he tried hard. During the early years of their married life, Ralph and Hazel moved often as Ralph searched for a job that suited him. His major interests had always been automobiles and motor competition. He had once raced in the modified division in the Seattle area — an involvement that satisfied his need for recognition and accomplishment. He wasn't great, but he was competitive. Later, when he and his bride settled in Las Vegas, he raced go-karts at local tracks, again without greatness, but with some success.

"I quit racing when Gary was born," says Ralph, "because I didn't want to risk being maimed or killed with a family to support. From then on, I devoted myself to my son."

Indeed, Ralph's devotion to Gary has always been more intense than that of an average father. You see, Ralph Wells is an alcoholic, a man cursed with a sickness that can be more harmful than most ailments that afflict mankind. But it is a sickness that can be cured; a problem that can be conquered; a weakness that can be strengthened. Ralph Wells found his strength in his son, Gary, and he conquered the problem. For all his adult life, it had kept him from succeeding. Now that he had a son, he could devote all his energies to the boy's success and, thereby, share it with him. So, to his relationship with his son, Ralph brought extraordinary devotion, a burning desire to succeed, and a deep love of motor competition. It was these that guided Gary Wells to his place above the average.

By the time he was three-and-a-half years old, he was racing quarter-midget race cars in the Las Vegas area.

"I had to sit him on several pillows," remembers Mr. Wells, "and he could only reach the gas pedal after I added two blocks of wood to it. But he did well against the competition who were all four to eight years old."

Actually, little Gary was six months too young to be competing in the quarter-midget class. But even then, Ralph Wells was in a hurry.

"You know, Gary was racing quarter-midgets before he could pronounce the word 'car,'" remembers Ralph with a smile.

During that time, Mr. Wells became Nevada Governor of the International Karting Federation, the sanctioning body for go-kart competition. The I.K.F. rules require that competitors be at least 12 years old to race. But Gary's father was not above "stretching" the rules just a little so that his son could begin racing earlier in Nevada. Gary started running go-karts when he was just seven. In races outside of Nevada, Ralph "exaggerated" Gary's age and usually got away with it. Despite his size and age disadvantages, Gary did sensationally well against all comers. By the time he was nine, he held three state championships — Nevada, Arizona, and Utah — and when he competed at the national finals that year in Quincy, Illinois, he was still three years younger than the minimum age for beginners in go-kart racing! No, he didn't win the national championship at Quincy — he didn't do well at all — but that is one of the few blemishes on his competition record.

When Gary was 10, Mr. Wells bought a Suzuki 80 street motorcycle so that he and his son could ride around on it together. Gary quickly learned how to ride the machine by himself. One day, the two attended a local motorcycle race as spectators. When it was over, Gary went out on the deserted track to ride the Suzuki. Soon another cyclist joined him and they began dicing and racing around the course. When the boy finally rejoined his father, Ralph studied his breathless, smiling face and he knew the motorcycle bug had bitten his son. And Gary knew it too.

He was 10 years old and he had all the go-kart trophies he could polish. So he gave up go-karting completely and devoted himself to motorcycle racing. And his father, who was his constant companion and his advisor, encouraged him.

"There are three cycle racing classes or divisions," explains Mr. Wells. "Novice, amateur, and expert. Gary was always smaller and lighter than the competition he faced. Some thought that his size was an advantage — that he could 'smoke' down the straightaways with ease. That was true, but he had problems 'muscling' through the corners.

"And he always had problems getting off the line because of his weight. He was only 80 pounds at 10 and 11 years old," continues Mr. Wells. "He didn't hit a hundred pounds till he was 13."

A proud smile spreads across Ralph Wells' face as he adds, "But within a year after he began cycle racing, he moved up to the expert division."

During this time, Mr. Wells was working as the service manager of an American Motors Dealership in Las Vegas. And every weekend, he and Gary traveled to wherever the motorcycle competition was best — California, Arizona, Utah. And in their path, they left the broken dreams of local heroes and a series of smashed track speed records. Traveling the open road together and winning almost everywhere they went drew Ralph Wells and his son even closer to each other. And in the course of their travels, they found a place where the cycle racing was best — Phoenix, Arizona. There the courses were tough, and the competition even tougher.

"I took a cut of $600 a month in my income to move us from Vegas to Phoenix," remembers Mr. Wells. "I left the service manager's job in Nevada and became manager of a Phoenix cycle shop. What's the difference? It was best for Gary and his racing. And that's all that matters."

Like Ralph, Hazel Wells has been caught up in the mad rush for Gary's success. There have been times when she wasn't happy about Gary's life on two wheels or the constant absence of her menfolk every weekend. But she went along with it all.

"Mom knew it was good for me to race," says Gary, "but she didn't like it when I started jumping."

And it wasn't long before cycle jumping became Gary's next objective. He won all the marbles in Phoenix cycle racing. He went undefeated in the Tucson, Arizona, area. And he was rarely beaten in California. By the time he was 13, the trophies of his cycle racing career were already collecting dust beside those he'd won in go-karts three years earlier. But he wasn't ready to leave motorcycles. The powerful two-wheelers had captured his imagination for good. Now he needed a new challenge for himself and his bike. And he knew just what it would be.

Before the Wells family moved from Las Vegas, Gary had watched Evel Knievel's famous conquest of the fountains at Caesar's Palace. That was almost four years earlier, but the memory of it had stayed fresh in his mind.

"I saw him crash at Caesar's Palace," remembers Gary, "and I thought it was neat. It didn't bother me at all."

Oh, it bothered him, all right. Not the crash, but the jump. It bothered him enough to want his own try at cycle jumping.

"We didn't think about jumping seriously," says Mr. Wells, "until Evel set his car-jump record at Ontario, California."

Everything that Ralph and Gary Wells do is a "we" effort. And it's been that way since Gary was born. In his conversation, Ralph Wells sometimes gives the impression that he and his son ride that motorcycle — and race it and jump it — double. And if it wouldn't slow them down, they probably would.

"We're poor people," says Ralph Wells, "and things have never been easy. When we moved to Phoenix, we lived in a small camper truck and we stayed with friends until we managed to get a little house in town. But my son is succeeding at what he loves best. That's all I want."

Gary Wells became a cycle jumper at 14. It took long hours of practice and hundreds of miles of cycling. It took clean living and daily exercise to strengthen his young muscles. It took total dedication and constant sacrifice. It took more than a man-sized measure of guts and talent. And it took his father's devotion and his mother's understanding. Cycle jumpers aren't born; they're made.

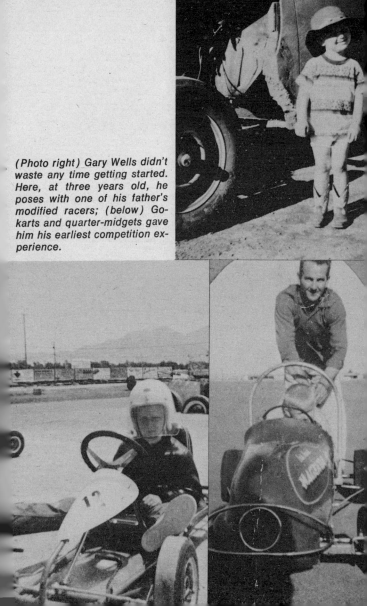

(Photo right) Gary Wells didn't waste any time getting started. Here, at three years old, he poses with one of his father's modified racers; (below) Go-karts and quarter-midgets gave him his earliest competition experience.

(Photo right) By the age of 12, Gary was displaying cycle racing trophies and the peace sign that became his symbol; (below right) By the time he was 10, he'd won all the trophies he could polish in go-kart competition; (below) Here, at 15, he shows his jumping bikes to family friend, Susan McElynn.

Photo by: Marshall Spie

(Photo below top) Although Gary's never been seriously injured jumping, he has been hurt racing cycles. He was unconscious for 10 hours after a racing wreck in 1969; (below bottom) At 12, Gary, right, held the Number 1 license plate in Phoenix cycle racing. That's Mr. Wells on Gary's back-up bike, Number 2.

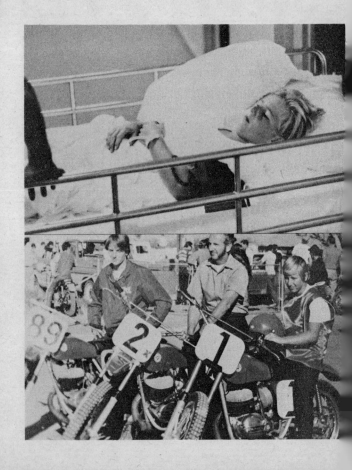

(*Photo right*) *Last minute instructions from Mr. Wells before a jump;* (*below top*) *Gary has always had to work at developing himself and staying in shape for cycle competition;* (*below bottom*) *Gary leads on number 102. Racing is his first love, but he's had to quit to be a cycle jumper.*

Photo by: Marshall Spiegel

Photo by: Marshall Spiegel

11th *CHAPTER*
Wells' Spoken Words

(Above left) The Wells family,
father Ralph, mother Hazel, Gary,
and his Montesa; (above right)
Gary and a girl friend.

GARY WELLS has always been shy and reserved. He doesn't smile easily. And when he
does, it's rarely the smile of a teenager without
care. On subjects that interest him, he can be
outspoken and conversant. But he seldom
wastes words. He has firm opinions on a variety of subjects, most of them related to
motorcycles.

"Cycling can be a great sport for everyone," says Gary. "A lot of kids should take cycle safety in school if it's offered. They'd learn to great deal. And it certainly should be offered in more schools. As for helmets, everyone should wear one when cycling. Anything that will reduce injuries has got to be good. A helmet could save a cyclist's life that one time when he goes down . . . and everybody goes down on a bike some time or another. Me, I want my helmet on all the time when I'm on a bike."

When the conversation gets around to Evel Knievel, Gary is quick to speak. Some of what he says is slightly tinged with jealousy. But that's understandable. Gary and his father are in a hurry. And Evel Knievel is already at their destination. Nevertheless, Gary has a great deal of respect for the King of the Stuntmen. He won't admit it publicly, but the kid recognizes Knievel's ability and showmanship.

"I read that Evel broke his hand or something in a jump recently," said Gary once. "I don't see how he could have. He must be made of glass."

Satisfied that he had "needled" the champion enough with that comment, he continued, "I've seen most of his jumps. I think he's a great showman and a great promoter. I envy his promotional ability especially. I thought the movie about him was kind of overdone. But I wish Evel had played the part himself . . .

"He says he's going to jump over the Snake River Canyon, but he keeps putting it off. Well, if he ever does, I'll jump over the London Bridge in Lake Havasu, Arizona. I don't know about that canyon jump. He may just be trying to destroy himself."

Although the kid often shows resentment for Knievel and the things he's said about Gary in public, he never misses an opportunity to study the King's style and form. And sometimes, he even dares to criticize it.

"Good jumping form means that you have to 'plane' your bike — fly level — while you're in the air," explains Gary. "Then when you touch down on your rear wheel — you must land on the rear wheel first — you don't get as strong an impact. No wonder Evel crashes so much! He's always at an upward angle in the air. And it's harder to control your landings that way."

As Gary's career developed, he made more and more public appearances. And from them and the exposure to people and places, he learned much about being a showman and a human being. He and his parents traveled from one performance to the next by truck, towing behind them a small but comfortable camper trailer in which they spent the nights.

When he wasn't busy, Gary began analyzing his life and what he wanted it to be.

"A lot of people think I'm a masochist," he said one day while lounging in the camper, "but if I'm going to get killed, it's going to happen. And I'd rather have it happen doing something I love . . ."

"Do you worry about the danger?" asked a visitor.

"No, I don't worry about it at all," replied Gary. "You know, cycle racing, that's really dangerous. I was run over once in a race in California by three bikes and I was unconscious in the hospital for 10 hours. I didn't worry about the danger then, and I'm not worried about it now."

Although cycle racing is the only way Gary has ever been injured seriously, it remains his first love. It is what he wants to do with his future. And he'd also like to continue his education.

"I'd like to travel and race," he explains. "With the help of a tutor, I'd like to finish the equivalent of high school. I quit at the end of the eighth grade to go on the road as a professional jumper. Now, I'm beginning to realize how important education is. When I left school in Phoenix, I didn't think I'd be talking on television and meeting so many important people.

"I'm in this jumping business for the money. Once I'm fixed, I can afford to race without working," he adds, "That's what I really want. I also plan to build a nice house for my folks as soon as I can. Maybe in Phoenix or Houston ... Then I'd like to buy a cycle shop so we always have something coming in."

Because of his jumping commitments, Gary is unable to race motorcycles, even for fun. If he were hurt prior to a jumping appearance, he'd have to break his contract and that would be expensive. So he plans his jumps, does his exercises, visits the neighbors at the trailer parks where the family stops each night, and he dreams of the day when he can quit jumping and race his motorcycles.

Ask him about his future and he'll give you his standard answer: "I plan to go on jumping a couple of years and making as much money as I can. Then I want to start racing cycles again.

"I get bored with stuff that's too easy," he continues. "If this got too easy, I'd quit now — but only if I had enough money first."

He's only been at it for a year, and already he speaks about quitting, about doing something else. Some people have said that the kid won't last. Except for some minor bruises at his big jump in Phoenix, he's never been injured. When he is — and the odds are that someday soon he will be — the skeptics are certain he'll quit. But his attitude toward crashing and the injuries that will inevitably result doesn't sound like that of a quitter.

"If I make a mistake, I know it's crash time — and it's hospital time," he says. "But the human body is a lot more durable than you think. It can take a lot before it dies."

It sounds like Gary Wells will go on jumping until the family purse is fat enough to suit him. Or until he becomes enchanted with another challenge he enjoys more. Or until he is hurt so badly that he is no longer physically capable. But he'll never quit a loser.

As Gary approached his sixteenth birthday recently, Ralph took stock of his son's size and weight. The kid once heard himself called a "shrimp" by some spectators at one of his appearances. True, until he sprouted recently, he was small. But he's no shrimp anymore. He's grown to 5 feet 8½ inches and he's filled out to 135 pounds on a trim, but strong frame. He wears his hair long and his baby face has changed to mature, well-chiseled features. Outside of motorcycles, Gary's only real interest is girls. And the girls find him as attractive as he finds them. His interest in the opposite sex is developed beyond his years.

"If I'm not riding my bikes," he says, "I'm

dating girls. But mostly, I enjoy anything on wheels, including my unicycle."

With his uncanny sense of balance, Gary is a superb unicycle rider, capable of riding and maneuvering the strange, single-wheeled device as well backward as he does forward.

Ralph Wells is not only Gary's father, but he's also his manager, coach, press agent, trainer, and best friend. No one knows in which capacity Ralph was serving when he said recently, "Sometimes cycle jumping appears so simple that Gary feels guilty about taking the spectators' money. But for him, it's that easy."

Then he added, "But it didn't get easy without hard work. Until we went on the road, Gary used to ride all day, every day in the desert. He's still too young to have a driver's license. He has four Montesas, and he rides them to death in the desert where it's legal. Even now, he rides daylight to dark whenever possible. And he's been lifting weights religiously for years. He started when he was racing so that he'd be strong enough to lift his bike if he went down in competition.

Gary's mother, Hazel, has her own thoughts about what has happened in her son's life.

"I think it's fine that Gary is jumping now, and jumping successfully," she once said. "I'll be more worried about him when he gets his driver's license and rides on the street. I think he's safer jumping because he knows what he's doing and because it's something he wants to do.

"He thinks his mother doesn't worry at all," she continued. "He even said so just the other day on the Mike Douglas television show. But I do! Then I always figure he could be doing worse things . . ."

Gary sums up the family's feeling this way:

"I take jumping as a job. No, I'm not afraid of it. If I were, I couldn't do a good job. I don't fear it at all. Actually, it's a lot of fun. I enjoy doing it. Look, instead of smoking grass, I jump cars! And I get paid for it besides!"

There have been those who can't understand how his parents can allow Gary Wells to risk his life in so dangerous an endeavor as cycle jumping. Several times, he's been barred from appearing at some places because of the objections of local officials or because of antiquated laws designed to protect minors. After all, he *is* just a kid. But he's a kid with a special combination of talent and courage; a burning desire to achieve his goals; and a genuine love for what he's doing. And he's been blessed — or cursed, depending on your point of view — by parents who understand.

12th CHAPTER

Cycling from Boredom

EVERY SCHOOL HAS THEM, that small group of students who just aren't interested in learning. They usually find seats in the back of their classes. Some daydream. Others disrupt those around them. Some are older and bigger than their classmates. Others are different only in their interests and objectives. Their grades are never good. And their progress is always limited. At the Paradise Valley Schools in Phoenix, Arizona, Gary Wells was a charter member of this group.

128

Although he may have been slightly older than his classmates, he was smaller than most of them. Sometimes he was disruptive, but usually he was just preoccupied, lost to education by thoughts of motorcycles and cycle racing.

At the Greenway School, which Gary attended, his eighth grade English teacher, Mr. Robert Quay, refused to lose him to the group of the disinterested. He learned of Gary's love of cycling and he used it to gain Gary's attention and to reach him. In September of 1971, after Gary had completed the eighth grade and left school to go on the road, Mr. Quay wrote to one of the editors of SCHOLASTIC SCOPE magazine about Gary. Here, in part, is that letter:

> Dear Sir:
>
> Enclosed are some current articles featuring a teenager who is not only a credit to the fine sport of motorcycling, but is also a tremendous credit to the "now" generation of teenagers.
>
> Gary is a fine person and I am very proud to have been associated with him for the past year. His entire life is centered on motorcycles. Every reading and writing assignment he received in my class (eighth-grade English) was concerned with motorcycles. Should it have been otherwise? Never!!
>
> I purchased paperbacks, magazines, and newspapers which involved motorcycles and made them available to Gary for use in the classroom. In spite of warnings I received from several of his

previous teachers to "watch out for Gary Wells," he never gave me a moment of trouble, because he was too busy doing something he enjoyed. He had no reason to be bored with English.

As an educator, I am convinced that we need to make school as relevant as possible in the life of each student. . . .

Sir, I take no credit for Gary's sudden success and subsequent fame, and I seek no personal benefit from my association with him, but I do hope your publication will see fit to spotlight this teenager, who is a prime example of what a person can do if he establishes a goal and strives with all his being to reach it.

His story should be a challenge and an inspiration to teenagers, as well as adults, everywhere.

From the viewpoint of educational philosophy, he serves as an example of what can be done with a potential problem student (because of boredom) when we make an honest effort to discover the interests of each pupil, furnish, if possible, materials related to that interest(s), and allow the student to pursue his areas of interest, instead of being limited to class-wide materials which may not interest him in the least.

Sincerely,
Robert Quay

True, Gary Wells was a "potential problem student." He never cared for the regimentation of the classroom. School subjects bored him. By that time, motorcycles had become his whole life. Fortunately for him, some of his teachers, like Mr. Quay, recognized his total involvement with cycling and did what they could to merge their subjects with Gary's interests.

After he left school, Gary's only education came from exposure to new people and places. It was an eye-opening experience for a fourteen-year-old.

Ralph Wells is not happy that Gary can no longer attend school. Because of their busy travel schedule, public school would be out of the question. However, both Gary and his father recognize the need to continue the young daredevil's education.

"Gary is supposed to have a tutor right now," said Ralph late in the summer of 1972. "And he will as soon as we get back to Houston."

At that time, they were preparing for Gary's three-day appearance at the huge Canadian National Exhibition in Toronto, Canada. When that appearance was completed, it was their plan to return to Houston, a city they had learned to love during Gary's performances at the Astrodome; to leave the show circuit for a while; to rest; and to take stock of Gary's career and his future. Because of Gary's success as a cycle jumper and the attention it has brought him, they feel that it is more important than ever that he continue his education. Unfortunately, he cannot be a cycle-jumping star and a student at the same time. And part of his appeal as an attraction and as a daredevil is his age. So the Wells family has had to sacrifice Gary's high school years so that he could continue as a professional jumper. Gary Wells will never know the life of a normal teenager. That is part of the price he must pay to pursue his career. And it is a high price indeed.

Not only was Gary deprived of the normal classroom experience, but he also lost the friendships of youth. The few friends his own age he knew in Phoenix were never really close. Although Gary is a likable boy, he's always been too involved with motorcycles to be a good friend to anyone. There's an old adage: "To have a friend, one must be a friend." So Gary Wells grew from boyhood to teen-age never knowing real friendship. And the few buddies he had were left behind for his professional career.

On the road, he enjoys the admiration of his fans. The girls — his age and older — love him. And the boys envy him. But his only friends remain his parents and his Montesa. There's no time for others. Gary Wells is only 15 years old and already he has grown accustomed to the painful loneliness of a professional entertainer.

Back in Phoenix, the guys at the Valley Cycle Shop haven't forgotten Gary. It was there that he received his earliest help and sponsorship. And it was there that he enjoyed the camaraderie of others who share his love of motorcycles. Even today, after Gary and his folks have left thousands of miles between themselves and Phoenix, the guys at Valley Cycle still know where he is; where he's been; how he's done; and where he's heading. Gary Wells is still their boy. He always will be.

To be a teenage cycle jumping star requires determination, courage, and sacrifice. Few spectators who watch the kid on his flying bike ever realize what he's had to give of his life to be where he is.

Photo by: Marshall Spiegel

Gary and his Mom are very close. That's one of the family's two boxers.

Photo by: Marshall Spiegel

It's not difficult to pick Gary out of this starting line. He was always the first one away.

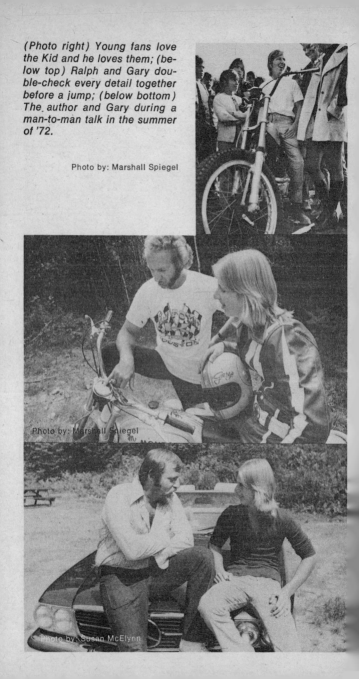

(Photo right) Young fans love the Kid and he loves them; (below top) Ralph and Gary double-check every detail together before a jump; (below bottom) The author and Gary during a man-to-man talk in the summer of '72.

Photo by: Marshall Spiegel

Photo by: Marshall Spiegel

Photo by: Susan McElynn

(Photo right) The Kid's machines topped by his 250 Montesa; *(center)* the Gremlin and the custom trailer that haul his bikes; and *(bottom)* the rental truck and camper-trailer that serve as home when the family is on the road.

Photos by:
Marshall Spiegel

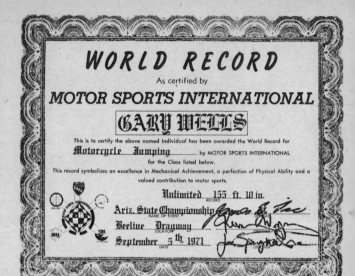

WORLD RECORD

As certified by

MOTOR SPORTS INTERNATIONAL

GARY WELLS

This is to certify the above named Individual has been awarded the World Record for

Motorcycle Jumping by MOTOR SPORTS INTERNATIONAL
for the Class listed below.

This record symbolizes an excellence in Mechanical Achievement, a perfection of Physical Ability and a
valued contribution to motor sports.

Unlimited 155 ft. 10 in.
RECORD

Ariz. State Championship
NAME OF EVENT

Beeline Dragway
LOCATION

September 5th, 1971
DATE

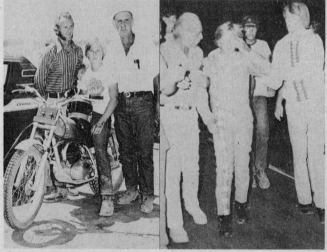

(Top) The official certificate of Gary's greatest jump; (above left) Ralph and Gary pose with actor Keenan Wynn before the record-setting jump in Phoenix; (above right) Gary was shaken by his spill after that jump, but not seriously hurt.

13th CHAPTER
The Kid's Machines

Photo by: Marshall Spiegel

LIKE EVEL KNIEVEL, Gary Wells is a lover of fine machinery. The difference is that the master of motorcycle jumping can afford to own the cars, trucks, and cycles he desires. The kid can only dream about them. But it won't be long before he has his dream car, a Chevrolet Corvette. Talk automobiles with the young daredevil, and you'll quickly learn that, as far as he's concerned, the 'Vette is the only car to own. Until he is old enough to have a driver's license (which will come on his sixteenth birthday in some states), he can only dream about driving any car.

It is ironic that Gary cannot yet legally drive on public streets even though he has been competing in motor competition for almost 13 years. But the law is the law, and he respects it; that is, most of the time. Somewhere in Houston (or is it Phoenix?), there's a '72 Gremlin collecting dust in a parking lot. It's a car that came into the Wells family a while back. Ralph used it to tow the handsome, two-cycle trailer he had built for hauling Gary's bikes to local tracks. And Hazel used it for shopping and errands. But there were times when Junior couldn't resist his strong urge to drive it off into the night. Since they've been on the road, Gary's been unable to do any driving — legal or otherwise. By the time he and the Gremlin are reunited, he'll have a driver's license. And he'll probably start shopping for that Corvette.

A large Chevrolet truck now serves as conveyance and warehouse for the Wells family. Rented from E-Z Haul on a long term basis, the Chevy is large enough to hold the ramps, tools, covers, and paraphernalia needed for Gary's performances. It also houses his motorcycles, two or three jumping Montesas and a couple of small-bore fun bikes, and his unicycle.

A small, comfortable camper-trailer is towed behind the Chevy truck. It serves as home while the family is on the road and it is Mother

144

Hazel's domain. Although she tries to keep the tiny rooms tidy, Ralph and Gary make it impossible. Ralph uses the camper as his office. Gary uses it as his dressing room. And both of them dart in and out of it dozens of times each day, leaving in their wakes everything from helmets and leathers to briefcases and newspapers. The truck-camper combination is a far cry from Evel Knievel's $140,000 custom-built Kenworth tractor-trailer, but it gets the job done for the Wells family for the time being.

Of course, the most important machine in the kid's life is his jumping bike. Much of his cycle racing success was achieved on Kawasaki motorcycles. But when the time came to jump, he chose Montesa, a Spanish-built motorcycle with less fame and less reputation than even he himself enjoyed. But he made the choice after a careful study of all the bikes capable of serving his needs. Why he selected a Montesa is something only Gary can explain. He says they feel "right" to him; that he's confident on them; and that he knows them best. And after all, it's his neck. Ralph recognizes the necessity for Gary to make his own choice in cycles and he does not interfere. Because Montesa is a small company with limited production for the United States market, they offer little financial help and sponsorship to Gary.

145

But they enjoy their greatest exposure and publicity from his performances on their machines. Evel Knievel says he loves the Harley-Davidson bikes he uses because "they're the best in the world." He rarely mentions the thousands of dollars of sponsorship he receives annually from Harley-Davidson for riding their machines. Gary Wells, on the other hand, claims he'd use a Montesa even if he had to pay for his show machines himself. Yet, an occasional gift bike is all the real support he gets from Montesa. But Gary and Ralph are beginning to recognize the need for company sponsorship and they are now looking for a cycle manufacturer who will come across with some money as well as the bikes Gary needs to perform. When they find one, Gary's marriage to Montesa will be over.

The family's expenses are very high. Items like Gary's $300,000 life-insurance policy and the mileage charges on their rented truck are essential costs of their business, but they take a big chunk out of the profit. Without sponsorship, they will not be able to afford the long climb to stardom.

The machine to which Gary owes his present success is Montesa's Cappra 250-MX. Except for special tires and a few tuning tricks, the bikes Gary jumps are 100 per cent stock right down to the standard spokes. Here, translated from the Spanish, are the specifications for the Cappra 250-MX as they appear in the owner's manual:

The two-stroke monocylinder engine measures 247.69 cc. with a bore of 72.5 mm. and stroke of 60 mm. Its brake power is 34 hp at 6,500 rpm and ignition is made through a flywheel magneto-alternator.

The engine is seated over a frame fabricated with steel pipes, mutually and electrically bonded and welded, and finally forming an assembly of great strength, stout and perfect handling.

The front suspension is of the telescopic fork type and the rear, one of swinging arms over clastic bushes which do not require any lubrication with double effect hydraulic dampers of adjustable starting charge.

The carburetor (AMAL) has a diameter of 32 mm. and takes air through a paper air filter located under the seat and easily accessible.

The gearbox is of five speeds in "cascade" and constant take-up pinions, which coupled to the steel multiple disk clutch in oil bath and regular tension springs, makes an assembly of great smoothness and high performance.

The brakes are of internal expansion (180 mm. diameter rear; 130 mm. diameter front) anchored by means of reaction bars.

The driven toothed gear of the rear wheel is mounted over clastic bushes fully insulated from the heat generated in the brake assembly.

Motorcycle experts will tell you that the Montesa is a well-built machine that is powered competitively for its class. Gary Wells will tell

147

you it is the best jumping bike he knows. Except for some loosened spokes, he has encountered no real difficulty with his Montesas either in practice or in his 18 public performances. And that's a rather good testimonial.

As time goes on and Gary Wells grows in stature as a cycle jumper, the machines that play such an important role in his life — motorcycles, cars, trucks, and campers — will probably be more impressive than they are right now. At present, he must make do with what he has, but he still seems to be getting the job done.

A rare photo of Gary during a practice jump prior to an early professional appearance.

14th CHAPTER

Struggle to Succeed

CYCLE JUMPING is no easy profession. Evel Knievel, the King of the Stuntmen, faced numerous obstacles when he originated the

"sport." Imagine him trying to convince a promoter or raceway owner that people would actually pay good money to see him jump his bike over a bunch of cars. Then he had to sell them on his ability to accomplish the feat without killing himself! Gary Wells has faced many of the same problems. It's true that Knievel, the King, had opened the door for the kid. By the time Gary was ready to do his stuff in pub-

lic, raceway owners and show promoters knew all about cycle jumping. Even the fans were "experts" on the subject, most of them educated by the "Evel Knievel" motion picture. But Gary Wells had an additional problem — he began when he was only 14.

Some states have laws to protect minors like Gary from participating in dangerous activities. For example, until he is 16, Gary is not permitted to perform in the states of New York or New Jersey. Even in his home state of Arizona, Gary was met with legal resistance in the form of "child endangerment" ordinances that prohibited him from performing. However, he was permitted to appear publicly in Arizona if he did so without receiving a fee. In other words, the same ordinances that stopped him from jumping for money permitted him to perform if he did so for charity. Whether the kid was being paid to jump or not, he always faced the possibility of breaking his neck. This tended to sour both Gary and his parents on the credibility of such legislation.

After his first two appearances at Beeline Dragway in Phoenix, Gary and his father went on tour. He successfully completed 14-car jumps at each performance and he drew large crowds wherever he appeared. In Denver, Colorado, the space was adequate and the performance was flawless. In Marion, Ohio, and

Chicago's U.S. 30 Dragway, Gary again thrilled large crowds of spectators. The constant push of road travel to strange places and new climates eventually got to him and he became sick on the tour. The doctors diagnosed it as mononucleosis, an ailment that weakens its victims and lingers for a long time in the body.

By December 12, 1971, Gary had beaten the bug, regained his strength, and was ready for another appearance in Phoenix, this time at Beardsley Raceway just outside of town. Beardsley owner Sonny Speilman is a close friend of Ralph Wells and his dusty little motorcycle track out in the boondocks needed a boost, an attraction to bring the fans in. After the attention Gary had received from his previous appearances in the Phoenix area, he was notified that Arizona law prohibited him from jumping in public because of his age, unless he did so for charity. So with Sonny Speilman's help, Gary and Ralph arranged to perform for the benefit of the Save-A-Child League, a non-profit Arizona organization dedicated to the education of poverty-stricken youngsters. Gary cleared 15 cars with ease that bright Sunday afternoon as an added attraction to the regularly-scheduled motocross events. Gary's old racing foe, Byron Boaz, won the feature race. And Gary won the hearts of the crowd with an outstanding performance

153

It was a full month before Gary jumped again, this time at the Houston Astrodome. And this time, he received a large fee. Prior to the performances — a 14-car jump on Friday, January 14, 1972, and a 15-car jump the following night — he spent several days making public appearances and enjoying great publicity.

His 14-car jump on Friday evening was spectacular. Like Evel Knievel, Gary complained afterwards about the cramped takeoff and landing room in the Astrodome. Although the "Dome" is more than adequate for most sporting events, it wasn't designed for motorcycle jumping. But then, no indoor arena has been.

Almost a year before Gary's appearance at the "Dome," Knievel had thrilled a Texas crowd with his sensational performances. But the fans loved the kid from Arizona just as well.

In his second performance, on Saturday, January 15, 1972, Gary cleared 15 cars and claimed a new indoor world's record. He also claimed a larger total audience for the two-day appearance than had been drawn by the master. Estimates of the crowds vary. Some say Evel drew 86,000 for his two-day appearance. He says it was 99,000. Some say Gary drew 91,000. He says it was more like 100,000. In any case, the King and the kid both filled the huge arena to the rafters.

154

"Houston was good to us," remembers Ralph Wells. "They really loved Gary. Since then we think of it as home. Someday we'll probably settle there."

From the glamour and professionalism of Houston, the Wells family moved on to Navasota, Texas, for a jump over 15 "battered" stock cars. Gary doesn't count that as one of his more memorable appearances, although his jump was long, straight, and true, and the Navasota folks received him well.

Several months passed before Gary received another booking. The family spent the time in the Houston area, with Ralph promoting and Gary preparing.

Then came the state fair at Brockton, Massachusetts, a five-day appearance with a jump each night. The money from Houston and Navasota was dwindling. And Gary was fit and eager to perform. He jumped first on June 30, setting the pace for his appearance at Brockton by clearing 15 cars and landing well down the landing ramp. He successfully repeated the feat the following two nights. On July 3, the skies over Massachusetts dumped heavy rain on the Brockton fairgrounds and a frustrated Gary Wells announced to a very disappointed audience that he would be unable to perform for them that night. But on July 4, he made it up to the large holiday

155

crowd by flying higher and farther over the 15 cars than he had in his previous performances.

The kid wasn't paid for his next appearance, not in money anyway. But he wouldn't have missed it for the world. Three weeks after Brockton, on an uphill macadam surface, a closed-off side street in Philadelphia, Pennsylvania, he cleared 15 cars. Except for a crowd of non-paying onlookers, his only audience was the television film crew for the Mike Douglas Show. It was Gary's first appearance on national television and his reward for the jump was invaluable publicity.

From Philadelphia, the Wells family headed to Monticello Raceway, a large trotting-horse track in Monticello, New York, where Gary was booked to jump on August 5. That appearance was cancelled by raceway officials when they learned of the New York State law that prohibits minors from performing dangerous feats publicly.

On Tuesday, August 22, Gary arrived at the Iowa State Fair for a two-day appearance.

"I cleared 15 cars both nights in Iowa," reported Gary afterward, "but I really wasn't happy with the crowd. Sonny and Cher were appearing at the fair at the same time and they outdrew me. I guess more folks know about them and about good singing. Frankly, if I wasn't busy jumping, I would have gone to see them myself."

Gary had only one day of rest before his next appearance, a three-day contract at the Canadian National Exhibition in Toronto, Canada. That appearance was his first outside of the United States. Not only did it give him international status as a performer, but it taught him a painful and expensive lesson about being a businessman.

15th CHAPTER

Gary Jumps
in Canada

IT WAS FIVE O'CLOCK in the morning before Gary and Ralph Wells were satisfied that their ramps were properly positioned for Gary's performances at the Toronto Fairgrounds. They had spent the day, Thursday, August 24, traveling from their previous engagement in Iowa to Toronto and they were both dog tired. But the Canadian National Exhibition (C.N.E.) is a major show, one of the largest annual fairs in North America, and it was a good booking for Gary. Naturally, they wanted everything to be just right. The

C.N.E. has a tradition of providing the most exciting and the newest circus and daredevil talent available. The 1972 show, which ran from August 16 to September 4, proved to be one of the best ever. Aerial, trapeze, and animal acts as well as unbelievable stunts thrilled the huge Canadian crowds each night. And for three days, from August 25 through 27, Gary Wells was featured as the final act of the night. For the kid, it was a good spot in good company.

The jump over 15 vehicles which Ralph and Gary planned was no more challenging than similar jumps Gary had made on other tours. But the stopping distance at Toronto was very short, approximately 90 feet, which was not nearly enough for a safe, comfortable stop from a takeoff speed of more than 80 miles per hour. It was even shorter than the space had been indoors at the Astrodome in Houston. And it worried Gary that first day.

The jump was set on a small paved-oval track. Beyond Gary's landing ramp, the run-off road ran directly into the end of the straightaway before the track curved sharply. And Gary's straightest escape route pointed dangerously close to the grandstands. A gate at the far end could be kept open for each of his jumps in case he was unable to stop his Montesa, but it would still be tight.

Friday, August 25, was a hot, humid day

160

in Toronto, but darkness brought clear skies and cooling breezes. Dressed in an elegant set of white leathers with blue stars and stripes, Gary Wells prepared for his first Canadian performance, scheduled for 10:30 p.m. At 9 o'clock, while the crowd's attention was centered on several aerial acts, Ralph Wells supervised the setting of his son's ramps on the darkened front straightaway. Fifteen cars and trucks from a local Ford dealer were parked neatly side by side between the ramps. A new set of ramp covers adorned with large, theatrical banners bearing Gary's name emblazoned in bold letters dressed up the ramps. Ralph Wells wore blue custom-made coveralls with "Gary Wells" embroidered in large letters within a white star on the back. The takeoff and landing ramps wore fresh coats of white paint. And Gary's Montesa, one of several of his jumpers, was specially painted and decorated. The Wellses had come to Canada to show their best. It had been only a year since Gary's first public appearance, but the kid who came to Canada looked and performed like a seasoned professional.

As Gary studied the jump, he said, "I think I'll have to clutch and lock up the brakes in the air so I can get stopped in time."

As his act was announced over the loudspeaker, Gary still wasn't certain of the correct takeoff speed and, more importantly, he wasn't sure where he'd be landing.

After a brief interview on the microphone, the kid treated the crowd to an outstanding warm-up session with one-handed wheelies and backward riding. Then he took the microphone and made an announcement.

"Folks, I haven't really had enough time to prepare for this jump," he began. "We were setting up the jump until five o'clock this morning. So please bear with me. The stopping distance here is very tight. And we want to check everything once more. Thank you."

The crowd cheered wildly and then waited quietly while the kid fired his bike again. He made two passes at the takeoff ramp to check his speed, to be sure that his engine was running sweetly. And then he raced up the ramp and flew high into the Canadian darkness. In an instant his flight was over, and he landed smoothly just below the "X" marked on his landing ramp. He skidded slightly as he fought the Montesa down the ramp and then he brought it to a safe stop not far from the end of the run-off road. It had been a good jump, an exciting performance. And Gary deserved the cheers of the crowd. A large group of autograph-seekers, many of them near his own age, mobbed him as he dismounted in front of the landing ramp. The kid had closed that night's performance of the Canadian National Exhibition with real style.

The next night went equally as well. Just prior to Gary's jump, a loose lug nut on his engine cover caused a slight delay. While his father tightened it, Gary explained the problem to the large Saturday night crowd. Then he mounted his bike and flew again over the 15-car obstacle with ease. Hazel Wells broke down and cried quietly in her seat in the grandstand. But her eyes dried quickly once Gary was safe. His landing was shorter and smoother than it had been the previous night, and his performance was more confident.

To those who watched Gary perform, everything looked calm and trouble-free. But the Wells family was growing uneasy even then. They felt that they hadn't been treated hospitably by the people at the C.N.E. and they didn't trust them. Mrs. Wells collected Gary's appearance money immediately after his performance on both Friday and Saturday nights.

"Maybe I'll start my own show," said Ralph Wells while he was dismantling the ramps. "I'll collect my own troop of performers, like that kid on the unicycle over there. . . . Then we won't have to put up with the nonsense we've been getting here."

But Gary chose to let his father shoulder the problems.

"I'll see you later, Dad," he said when the ramps had finally been dismantled. "I'm going to see what the girls look like."

Dressed in jeans, boots, and a colored tee-shirt and looking much like any teenager in the crowd, Gary disappeared with a couple of newly-found friends into the gaiety of the brightly-lit fairway.

Sunday, August 27, 1972, was to be a day that Gary Wells and his parents would never forget. Scheduled to be his last performance at the C.N.E., Sunday found Toronto muggy and overcast. Although Gary's performances and the reception he received from the spectators had been good, he and his folks had grown increasingly more uneasy in Toronto. No one but them knew of the problems they were having with the exhibition officials and the promoters. Under the terms of their agreement, Gary's appearance money was to be paid to his mother immediately after each of his performances. And the bargain had been kept on both Friday and Saturday nights.

On Sunday, at 8:30 p.m. — just two hours before Gary was to jump — a slight drizzle began to fall on the fairgrounds. Neither Gary Wells nor his father are experienced businessmen. They aren't accustomed to dealing with the promoters who operate exhibitions like Toronto. They aren't familiar with legal contracts and how to read them. And they're new at the business of professional entertainment. Trusting that their contract at Toronto contained the same clauses as previous agreements made by their booking agents, Gary and Ralph assumed that they would be paid if Gary was prepared to jump, but was unable to do so because of inclement weather. Without looking at the contract and just to be certain that was the case, Gary took it upon himself to ask the exhibition manager if he would be paid in the event of a rain-out. An argument ensued and harsh words were exchanged.

When the time came for Gary's jump at 10:30, the rain had stopped and the skies were clear. Gary was ready, dressed in his leathers and mounted on his cycle. However, his ramps had not been set up and an announcement was made that Gary would not be making an appearance that night. The audience, many of whom had come just to see Gary Wells jump, sat in shocked amazement at first and then they booed and jeered wildly.

Gary stepped up on the announcer's stand, hoping for a chance to explain what had happened, and a large crowd of spectators gathered around him. But the microphone had been disconnected and he was frustrated in his attempt.

Whatever actually happened that night at the Canadian National Exhibition in Toronto is known only by those directly involved. In any case, the kid didn't jump that Sunday evening even though the rain had stopped. But he learned a little bit about how to deal with people; how to be a businessman; and how to hold his temper. And he got a taste of the seamy side of professional cycle jumping, a lesson that Evel Knievel had learned a long time ago.

Ralph and Gary loaded their ramps, hooked up their trailer, and headed back to Houston the next morning. Although they lost one night's appearance money, they had added a few more dollars to their bank account and they'd grown a little wiser about their strange business. After Toronto, it was time to rest for a while and then begin the search again for another engagement.

16th CHAPTER

Tomorrow the Moon

Photo by: Marshall Spiegel

IT'S BEEN EIGHT YEARS since Evel Knievel began teaching the world about long-range motorcycle jumping. His performances were received as unbelievable acts of daredeviltry. It wasn't until other men attempted to copy him that cycle jumping became a competitive sport. Today, as other jumpers perfect their abilities, the feat moves closer to becoming a truly competitive sporting event.

Many athletic endeavors popular today were born much the same way. Before there could be ski-jumping competition, someone had to jump on skis. Before there could be high-diving competition, someone had to dive from a great height. Before there could be weight-lifting competition, someone had to lift a great weight. And before cycle jumping can be recognized as a competitive sport, men like Evel Knievel and Gary Wells must make their marks in the pages of sports history.

What does tomorrow hold for Evel Knievel? There has been some talk that he is training his oldest son to follow in his footsteps. Whether Evel and Linda Knievel can stand by and watch one of their own in the dangerous business of cycle jumping is doubtful, but not impossible. Knievel himself has been a star too long; he's been hurt too often; and he's known too much of the problems of his business. Nevertheless, the time is drawing near when he will have to call it quits. His badly broken body will soon refuse to heal as it did when he was younger. If he is to remain prominent in the sport, he will have to do so by creating a new show, one featuring a younger cycle jumper. Perhaps his son will be ready when that time comes. Or perhaps he will take a talented young man like Gary Wells under his wing. Age will soon steal from Evel

Knievel the sharp reflexes and the precise timing essential to a successful cycle jumper. That is inevitable. But age can never take from him his superb sense of showmanship and the knowledge that he has gained through experience. If the King of the Stuntmen can walk away from his very last performance — if he can retire from active participation in one piece — he could become the driving force for perpetuating the sport that he originated. No one knows it better.

To those who know Knievel well, thoughts of his retirement and visions of him doing anything less than flying his Harley through the air are inconceivable. To predict Evel Knievel's long-range future, one must remember that the man is unique, and that his whole life has been completely unpredictable.

It would be safer to forecast Knievel's immediate future. Right now, his sponsors are paying him big money. He is in great demand for public appearances. The public will never know his name or his reputation better than it does right now. And his body, with its pain and scars, is still able to respond to his strong and reckless will. Thus, it's safe to guess that he will continue to jump for a while. He rescheduled his attempt to conquer the Snake River Canyon for July 4, 1973. He has dreamed and talked of that jump too long and too hard not to attempt it. And his colossal ego would never permit him to willingly leave the challenge untried. Chances are he will continue to make appearances as he has until the canyon attempt. If he is successful at the Snake River, he may begin dreaming of greater obstacles to conquer. If he fails, he will have lived and died as only a King of Stuntmen could.

What of Gary Wells and his future? The kid has proved that he can be a big-league cycle jumper. At present, he is the only real contender for Knievel's crown. In the year since his first public appearance, he and his father have learned much of what it takes to be showmen. The kid knows how to warm the crowd with carefully worded announcements. His pre-jump motorcycle antics have begun to show more and more professionalism. His form and style have developed a flavor of their own. And he has not yet attempted a distance that he has been unable to conquer successfully.

The feat of cycle jumping has been good to Gary Wells. He has known the admiration of spectators everywhere he's appeared. He's built a bank account greater than 10 boys his age who do lesser, more usual work. And he remains unbroken and unscarred after his first year as a professional and 18 public performances.

But the business of cycle jumping and the life it forces him to lead are beginning to tell on the kid. Like Knievel, Gary jumps for money primarily. But the adoration of the fans and the status of a celebrity have been additional motivation for both of them. It is understandable that such prominence at so tender an age has turned Gary's head. Yet, he could still survive without it. It is doubtful that Evel Knievel can ever forget the cheers of his fans. So, in Gary's case, he will go on jumping for money. As he gains more experience, chances are he will attempt greater distances. If he isn't seriously injured, the day may come when he will surpass the greatest marks set by the King, although it is unlikely that Knievel will ever admit that he'd been beaten by anyone.

Studying Gary Wells at the age of 15 leaves one uncertain. He does not yet show the spark of a great showman, but it may come. He does not yet indicate the strong desire to spend his life becoming a champion cycle jumper, but it too may come. He does not yet command huge appearance money because he still performs in the shadow of the King. Perhaps, when Evel Knievel leaves the sport, things will be better for Gary Wells. Right now, he will go on jumping, snatching every appearance offer he can get. He will continue to seek the sponsorship money that has not yet been offered. And he will pray for a challenge from

Evel Knievel, a chance for a show-down. But it will never come. As long as Knievel goes on jumping, regardless of the marks that are set, Gary Wells will be forced to settle for second best. The King has a head start of too many years, too many jumps, and too many fans. He's a legend, one that won't be forgotten easily.

Not only must Gary Wells look ahead at Evel Knievel, but he must also watch the young jumpers who now pursue him and his records. As more of them are successful, the sport of cycle jumping will undoubtedly receive the regulation it so badly needs. Hopefully, the day will soon come when record jumps are measured precisely, in footage, by a recognized sanctioning body. But right now, Evel Knievel and Gary Wells go on talking about jumping endless rows of cars; unbelievably wide canyons; and huge steel bridges. Of course, they are the first generation of cycle jumpers. Those who follow them tomorrow may even talk of jumping the moon.